NATIONAL PARKS OF ARIZONA & CALIFORNIA

STRESS-FREE GUIDE TO TRANQUIL RETREATS, SCENIC
HIKES, AND EXHILARATING ADVENTURES FOR
SINGLES, SENIORS, FAMILIES, AND PETS

CATICO TRAVELER, PH.D.

There are numerous helpful web resources that have been researched and included in this book. To access all links compiled per park click or scan below if you are previewing this book online. Book purchasers refer to this image towards the end after the conclusion.
URL: https://lady-dobeington-publishing.ck.page/89928385f8

Hyperlinks embedded throughout this book are underlined and italicized. Click directly on these links in the e-book to navigate directly to the corresponding websites. The resource links guidebook contains hyperlinks with the full URLs if you prefer to type the addresses into the web browser search bar yourself or for easy access with the print copy of the book.

CONTENTS

Introduction   9

CHAPTER 1: SOUTHWEST HIKING BASICS   13
What Is Hiking and Why Is It Beneficial?   14
Hiking in the Southwest   15
Trail Selection   16
Trail Difficulty Ratings in this Guide   17
Route Mapping and Safety Plan   18
Southwest Hiking Essentials   19

Part I
THE THREE NATIONAL PARKS OF ARIZONA

CHAPTER 2: GRAND CANYON NATIONAL PARK   23
Contact Information   24
Park Overview   24
Planning   25
Admission and Fees   26
Directions   27
Accommodations   28
Park Attractions   29
Top Hiking Trails – Locations, Specifications, Activities and
Sites   30

CHAPTER 3: PETRIFIED FOREST NATIONAL PARK
ARIZONA   41
Contact Information   42
Park Overview   42
Planning   43
Admissions and Fees   43
Directions   44
Accommodations   44
Park Attractions   45
Top Hiking Trails – Locations, Specifications, Activities and
Sites   46

CHAPTER 4: SAGUARO NATIONAL PARK   55
Contact Information   56
Park Overview   56
Planning   57
Admissions and Fees   58
Directions   58
Accommodations   59
Park Attractions   59
Top Hiking Trails – Locations, Specifications, Activities and
Sites   61

Part II
THE NINE NATIONAL PARKS OF
CALIFORNIA

CHAPTER 5: CHANNEL ISLANDS NATIONAL PARK   73
Contact Information   74
Park Overview   74
Planning   75
Admission and Fees   76
Directions   76
Accommodations   77
Park Attractions   78
Top Hiking Trails – Locations, Specifications, Activities and
Sites   79

CHAPTER 6: DEATH VALLEY NATIONAL PARK   89
Contact Information   90
Park Overview   90
Planning   91
Admission and Fees   91
Directions   92
Accommodations   93
Park Attractions   94
Top Hiking Trails – Locations, Specifications, Activities and
Sites   96

CHAPTER 7: JOSHUA TREE NATIONAL PARK   109
Contact Information   110
Park Overview   110
Planning   111
Admission and Fees   111
Directions   112

Accommodations   112
Park Attractions   113
Top Hiking Trails   115

CHAPTER 8: KINGS CANYON AND SEQUOIA NATIONAL
PARKS   127
Contact Information   128
Park Overview   128
Planning   129
Admission and Fees   130
Directions   130
Accommodations   131
Park Attractions   132
Top Hiking Trails – Locations, Specifications, Activities and
Sites   133

CHAPTER 9: LASSEN VOLCANIC NATIONAL PARK   147
Contact Information   148
Park Overview   148
Planning   149
Admission and Fees   149
Directions   150
Accommodations   150
Park Attractions   151
Top Hiking Trails – Locations, Specifications, Activities and
Sites   152

CHAPTER 10: PINNACLES NATIONAL PARK   163
Contact Information   164
Park Overview   164
Planning   165
Admission and Fees   166
Directions   166
Accommodations   167
Park Attractions   167
Top Hiking Trails – Locations, Specifications, Activities and
Sites   168

CHAPTER 11: REDWOOD NATIONAL AND STATE PARKS   177
Contact Information   179
Park Overview   179
Planning   179
Admission and Fees   180
Directions   180

Accommodations   181

Park Attractions   182

Top Hiking Trails – Locations, Specifications, Activities and
Sites   183

CHAPTER 12: YOSEMITE NATIONAL PARK   193

Contact Information   194

Park Overview   194

Planning   195

Admission and Fees   196

Directions   196

Accommodations   199

Park Attractions   201

Top Hiking Trails – Locations, Specifications, Activities and
Sites   202

Conclusion   213

References   219

INTRODUCTION

Remember taking road trips as a child and asking your parents, "Are we there yet?" every five minutes the moment you reached the end of your block? Between our youth and distance incognizance, it was natural to become impatient. As we aged we learned that things often take time; however, as technology advanced our modern era expectation became that everything is immediately available at our fingertips online. Success and happiness have become synonymous with instant gratification.

We chase one milestone after another constantly desiring more material possessions. Once upon a time we would have been content enjoying a coffee with friends, reading a book, taking a walk, or simply soaking up the sun. Today no time remains to enjoy life's simple pleasures. Aside from goals and aspirations, there are far too many responsibilities to stop and be mindful of the moment. Life becomes a blur of work and errands. We are never satisfied pursuing more money, a bigger house, or a fancier car.

So, what happens? We rush through everything and push ourselves beyond our limits. Endless seeking for the next best thing leaves us physically and mentally exhausted. Sadly, we rarely understand the impacts of our stress until it's too late. Those headaches, heartaches, and digestive issues are coming from somewhere!

Then the pandemic hit and life came to a screeching halt while households, schools, and businesses struggled to adapt to the new normal. Confined to our homes and isolated from life's bustle, we became bored, antsy, and depressed. Overnight we were forced to stop. And with this newfound time all many of us could do was think about what we were missing. The sheer loss we all experienced from our daily activities to interactions with family, friends, and coworkers made it clear that life is short, too short to be stuck in a rat race chasing the unattainable.

When remote schooling and work kicked in we were consumed by the changes, challenges, and compulsion for technology. Our quiet reflection on what we were missing in life became minimized.

 "We need to do a better job of putting ourselves higher on our own 'to do' list."

— *MICHELLE OBAMA*

I have struggled with generalized anxiety disorder since childhood, which necessitated coping mechanisms and creative outlets. Nature and hobbies helped me push through each day. While outdoors I felt at peace, especially with my older sister. As with older siblings, despite only being a few years my senior she considered herself the expert on *everything* and I was happy to follow her trail in or outdoors. However, as happens with most of us outdoor recreation like hiking and biking along with hobbies like dance classes and horseback riding were replaced with studies and career.

I was proud to earn my doctorate degree in molecular biology and become a full-time biology and biotechnology professor. I even achieved tenure, but at a time when I should have been downright joyful, I was more stressed and less physically fit than I had ever been. There was a nagging feeling that I needed something else in my life. I had no work-life balance, but like many I kept telling myself there was time… until COVID-19 hit in 2020.

Being cut off from human contact during the pandemic left me depressed. Then my sister became gravely ill and I had to isolate myself from her to protect her from infection. I hit rock bottom when I lost her to glioblastoma brain cancer in June 2020.

I know that I can't be the only one who has felt crushed over the past few years. We are bombarded with such negative media from gun violence and natural disasters to divisive politics and financial recession. We care for those who depend on us, young and old. We spend long hours in the office and bring work home as emails, texts, and calls come in at all hours. It likely has already started to take its toll on your physical or mental health, or both! You may soon wake up and realize that you are missing out on the true meaning of life. After all, no one lies on their deathbed wishing that they had worked more hours or bought better cars. They regret missing out on life experiences with loved ones.

I tried various remedies to free myself from the darkness and solitude I was stuck in with little success. I turned to yoga and meditation to find some inner peace, so much so that I completed 200 hours of study to become a certified yoga instructor and an additional 300 hours of advanced training. Later, I also completed meditation and breathwork certificates. While yoga provided a good diversion, it was only when I found my way back to nature that the shroud of depression finally started to lift fully because it put me back in touch with my inner child.

Heck, studies have shown that something as simple as a plant in a hospital, office, or school can reduce stress and anxiety. One specifically showed that patients recovering from gallbladder surgery with a view of trees tolerated pain better and were discharged sooner than those who only viewed a wall (_Delagran_, n.d.). Spending time in nature doesn't only heal; it has the power to restore our physical wellbeing, improve our mood, and add meaning to life. It helps remind us that we are only a small part of something much grander in the world.

It is challenging to strike a balance between work and recreation, technology and nature, but the benefits are exponential. Mother Nature dissolves stress helping us glean the benefits of physical activity while finding total relaxation. Nature allows you to clear your mind of everyday worries freeing up brainpower for perspective and self-reflection on your current life. Hiking leaves you rejuvenated and motivated. Can you say the same thing after working or running errands? My life partner and I regularly explore national park trails to disconnect from the chaos of daily life.

My dream is to help others discover the same love and passion for nature that we have, so more folks can discover the benefits that spending time outdoors provides for them and their families. Realize that taking a break from emails, text messages, and social media to slow down and unapologetically put yourself first is the ultimate way to live life. And together we can protect these natural resources for generations to come.

Ready to start your new life? There are 423 national park sites in the United States and its territories spanning 84 million acres. These include battlefields, historical sites, memorials, monuments, and parks. National parks contain extensive natural resources, and there are 63 of these spread across 28 states and 2 territories.

My motivation behind this book is for you to find the most in-depth information on Southwest national parks to glean the most out of your time and budget. This book covers the twelve stunning national parks of Arizona and California. Colorado, Nevada, New Mexico, and Utah will be covered in another book. That way you can focus on the book that has the parks you wish to visit rather than having a longer, more expensive version.

Normally planning a trip is stressful, which is ironic since we vacation to escape stress. How do you get there? Where do you stay? What sites should you see? Can you stay on budget? Have you ever returned from a trip feeling like you needed a vacation from your vacation? Not here! With the details in this book, the only thing you need to focus on is spending time with your friends and family or alone in peaceful solitude. It invites you to awaken your curiosity as you explore new areas and experience new activities before life passes you by!

We always say that we will do things tomorrow, but tomorrow is never given and time sneaks away from us. Seize the moment and start crossing these trips off your bucket list today! This comprehensive travel guide removes all the planning guesswork. While other guides may have more eye-catching maps and prettier pictures, they won't necessarily give the same peace of mind as knowing that you are fully prepared for travel and hiking.

It doesn't matter if you have never strolled through the countryside or if you are an expert hiker. There is guidance for all experience levels, highlights from each park, and even some of the best places to stay. We cover all the safety information and what you need to be fully prepared so that the only thing on your mind is what you sense in these breathtaking locations. With that in mind, our first chapter is all about the basics!

CHAPTER 1: SOUTHWEST HIKING BASICS

"I'm losing precious days. I am degenerating into a machine for making money. I am learning nothing in this trivial world of men. I must break away and get into the mountains to learn the news."

— *JOHN MUIR*

Inside bustling city offices where people exchange ideas might be where you expect to learn the most. However, as Muir said, a mountain excursion offers unimaginable education from self-discovery to culture and history.

To fully enjoy the hiking experience, safety and preparation must come first. Choosing a trail that is beyond your capability or forgetting to pack the essentials is a sure way to take the fun out of your adventures. But first, what exactly is hiking?

WHAT IS HIKING AND WHY IS IT BENEFICIAL?

Hiking is *not* synonymous with walking or trekking. While there are similarities, the distance and terrain set them apart.

Walking is done indoors on a treadmill, or outdoors through the city or suburbs, in parks, or through the countryside. Hiking is an outdoor walk on nature paths often with elevation changes associated with mountains. Terrains can also include valleys, canyons, forests, and peaks. Individual hikes may take half to a full day, or you can combine short hikes into a series of hikes. Trekking also involves walks in natural terrain, but the distance is generally longer lasting over a week.

Hiking benefits are numerous including exploring nature while nurturing your mental and physical health. Let's start with the cardiovascular system since heart disease is a leading cause of death in so many countries. Starting off with light hikes to raise the heart rate improves aerobic fitness. Over time, increase your hiking difficulty to condition your cardiac muscle and arteries. This can lower blood pressure and bad cholesterol along with improving glucose tolerance to increase sugar metabolism and decrease type II diabetes risk.

Our sedentary lifestyles and unhealthy diets often cause adipose tissue to increase while muscle and bone mass decrease. Aging results in similar concerns; however, hiking is a weight bearing exercise that burns fat and builds muscle and bone. It boosts balance and proprioception, which is how the mind processes the body's position and its movements in relation to objects and obstacles—think of stepping over rocks. With time, the brain gets better at balancing the body and judging obstacles as we maneuver around them.

Hiking increases our breathing rate, and therefore, oxygen flow to the brain which strengthens neuron connections. Stronger connections stimulate better brain function and even memory. So instead of feeling guilty about spending time away from your desk, embrace your hiking adventures which may enhance your productivity when you return to work.

More activity can enhance restful sleep leading to reduced stress and anxiety as well as improved overall mood. There is a link between morning sunlight and increased melatonin sleep hormone production at night, so get outside for an early hike! (Mead, 2008).

Nature removes everyday life stressors and calms the mind. Once you put your electronic devices away for a few hours, you can really start to be mindful of the present.

HIKING IN THE SOUTHWEST

It has been said that a picture is worth a thousand words, however, sometimes photos provide misrepresentations. A simple example: have you ever ordered an item online, but when it arrives you think how much larger it looked in the photos? This is not true for the Southwest as even the most beautiful photos don't do justice to the diversity and grandeur appreciated in person. Canyon tops reaching for the clouds offer breathtaking views as far as the eye can see; at the bottom, you can splash through creeks and peer upward at towering waterfalls. Additionally, you will find diverse, rugged terrain, hidden caves, deserts, and mountain ranges. This terrain is home to an equally diverse range of wildlife such as deer, elk, bighorn sheep, wild cats, bears, snakes, and falcons that have adapted to these environments.

The Southwest is brimming with history and culture. Here you can find some of the oldest ruins north of Mexico and enchanting cliff houses that are some of the oldest continuously inhabited homes in the United States. There are Spanish and Mexican influences, cowboys roaming the deserts, and art depicting tribal traditions.

With such cultural influences there is also an extraordinary range of cuisine. You can recharge your batteries with treats like chili cheeseburgers, huevos rancheros, or hearty stews. Local restaurants are proud to entice you with their homegrown fruits and vegetables. And these dishes can be washed down with craft brews or a crisp wine from one of the vineyards.

Whether you choose a single day's hike around one of the many attractions or decide to embark on a longer adventure through multiple national parks, there is no shortage of beauty, charm, and adventure waiting for you in the Southwest.

TRAIL SELECTION

When choosing a trail there are a few things to keep in mind aside from the difficulty rating examined in detail in the next section.

First, make an honest assessment of your physical abilities starting with your fitness and activity levels. You can quickly ruin a well-planned hike by choosing a trail that is too easy or difficult. An experienced hiker should select trails that challenge your abilities; however, if you are inexperienced or inactive, choose shorter, well-kept trails with less elevation.

Along with physical abilities consider any injuries or body parts that may start to ache after a while. My lower back is my weak spot and although I have strong legs, I must recognize my own potential limitations. If you are concerned about your fitness level, injuries, and/or joint issues start off with an easier route.

Weather influences the trail regardless of difficulty rating. Consider the difference between walking through the park on a hot afternoon and hiking for miles through the desert given its drastic temperature fluctuations. The average high temperature in the Southwest is 66.6°F and the average low is 37°F, although this can vary greatly depending on the location and season. Spring is generally an ideal time to enjoy warmer weather without brutal heat. While winter hiking through snow offers a whole new experience, it will be harder work, so again, probably not something to tackle during your first hike. The same applies to rain. Hiking in light rain can be refreshing, but heavier downpours pose a higher risk of slipping and injury. After significant rain or snow, a good rule of thumb is to increase a trail's difficulty rating by 1. So, a moderate trail on a dry day would become difficult in wet conditions.

Then there is the trail's condition. Easier trails are generally well maintained with wider paths and more signs. Aside from less signage, harder trails may have narrow, steep stretches with more obstacles like tree limbs or rocks to climb over.

Consider your safety above all else. There will be time to extend your hikes to go further and higher. Once you have gained experience you can start to explore more challenging trails, preferably in spring and fall during ideal conditions. In extreme weather conditions stick to familiar or slightly easier routes.

TRAIL DIFFICULTY RATINGS IN THIS GUIDE

There are various difficulty ratings for hikes, which can make it more challenging to decipher. The difficulty may also be partially subjective depending on abilities and experience. Many parks have their own ratings. Let's review a couple to get a better idea.

Hiking Project – 6 Difficulty Levels: (*Hiking Project*, n.d.)

- Easy – No obstacles and flat.
- Easy/Intermediate – Some uneven terrain but mostly flat.
- Intermediate – Moderate incline with uneven terrain.
- Intermediate/Difficult – Some rocks and roots with steep sections.
- Difficult – Steep with tricky terrain.
- Very Difficult – Very steep with potentially hazardous terrain.

Yosemite Decimal System – Classifies hikes *and* climbs, so most of the national park hikes fall into the first 3 groups: (*Valenti*, 2016)

- Class 1 – Easy hiking with minimal elevation and a few obstacles.
- Class 2 – More difficult hiking, some off–trail, and you may need to use your hands for support at times.
- Class 3 – Scrambling or climbing without a rope.
- Class 4 – Climbing with a rope.
- Class 5 – Technical climbing.

One final example gives more details regarding elevation and distance: (*Randonnée Aventure*, n.d.)

- Level 1 – Elevation: 500–1000 feet; Distance: 5–7 miles.
- Level 2 – Elevation: 1000–1500 feet; Distance 5.5–7.5 miles.
- Level 3 – Elevation 1500–2500 feet; Distance 6–7.5 miles.
- Level 4 – Elevation: 2500–3000 feet; Distance 7–9 miles.
- Level 5 – Elevation: 3000–5000 feet; Distance between 8 to 12 miles.

We will use a simple 3 level system for an overview of trail difficulties across different parks, but alongside this there will be details to help you judge the suitability for yourself and those hiking with you:

- Beginner – Suitable for most ages (toddlers to seniors) with a basic fitness level. 2 hours or less with even terrain and some accessible and wheelchair friendly routes. Since my partner has mobility issues using a cane or walker, I understand the importance of inclusivity.
- Intermediate – Suitable for those with a moderate fitness level with some hiking and exercise experience. 2–4 hours long with some moderate inclines and uneven terrain.
- Advanced – Suitable only for those with a high fitness level and sound physical health, preferably hiking regularly. Half day–all day or overnight with some steep inclines and tricky terrain containing obstacles.

For extra peace of mind, you can also check the trails with the national park you plan to visit as they often have detailed descriptions of difficulty ratings. Plus, with the knowledge you gain in this chapter you can better decide which trails are appropriate for you.

ROUTE MAPPING AND SAFETY PLAN

Now that you know a hike isn't equivalent to a walk it probably makes sense that you can't just grab your phone and keys to head out for some fresh air. Sticking with the safety theme there are a few preparations while still at home.

Before you confirm your route consider whether you are hiking alone or with others. Solo hiking can offer much needed peace and solace, however, it requires special planning since there is often safety in numbers. When hiking alone it is advisable to choose an easier trail that is well populated, especially if you are a beginner.

Once your route is planned, plot your detailed course on a printed map or map book. For overnight (or longer) hikes, mark where you will be staying each day. Do *not* stray from your plan so others can always find you. Share your itinerary with someone who *isn't* hiking with you and have an emergency plan whether you are hiking alone or with others.

If you get lost or separated from others, remain calm and breathe deeply to avoid panicking, which removes the brain's logical thinking. Stay put and recall any signs, markers, or landmarks that you saw on the trail. A pro tip is to look back every now and again on your path to gain a different perspective. The goal is always to find your way back to the main path. Even if your hiking partner(s) left the main path, don't try to follow them as there is no guarantee that they have stuck to the planned trail and may have diverted to look for you. Head back to your starting point or a prearranged meeting spot.

So, you have your route and the excitement is building, but there are still a few more things you need to take with you.

SOUTHWEST HIKING ESSENTIALS

These are the essentials that you should carry in a backpack or crossbody bag.

Navigation and Communication: While most smartphones have GPS, maps, and apps that help you navigate, the point of escaping into nature is to break free from these devices. Technology also fails, so bring a paper map and compass. A satellite phone provides coverage where cell phones don't.

Clothing: Dress in layers to manage your body temperature. Moisture wicking materials like polyester, nylon, fleece, and merino wool are better fabric choices than cotton, which dries slowly if you get it wet and has poor insulation. Pack a light raincoat, gloves, and hat even on a sunny day as weather conditions can change quickly.

Footgear: Comfortable and well sized hiking boots suited for your trail difficulty including traction devices for icy conditions such as ice cleats. Error on the larger side as your feet can swell when walking all day. Wear high quality moisture wicking socks that you don when purchasing your boots. Break in new boots around the house or at the local park, not on a hike.

Water: Plan for half a liter (about 2 cups) per hour. As you should never drink straight from natural sources, also carry water–purifying tablets/filters if you aren't going to boil it. Don't forget extra water if you are hiking with your pet!

Food: High calorie snacks like protein bars or trail mix along with pet food or treats if your four-legged friend is along for the trip. If you are out for longer than expected, these will provide you with energy.

First aid kit: Prescriptions, painkillers, antihistamines, plasters, bandages, medical tape, antibacterial wipes, antibiotic ointment, cotton balls, eye drops, hydrogen peroxide, tweezers, and scissors. For added peace of mind, I maintain my first aid and CPR (cardiopulmonary resuscitation) certification each year. Local American Red Cross offices along with fire stations or community colleges often offer these classes.

Environmental: Sunscreen, wide brimmed hat, and sunglasses, even in the winter as the sun's reflection off snow can cause snow blindness. Insect and bear repellent (effective on many mammalian species).

Light: High lumen, small flashlight, or headlamp in case you stay out after dark. Don't forget spare batteries or a USB cable and battery bank.

Multi–purpose tool or knife: Many uses in first aid, food preparation, or gear repair (can purchase a repair kit too).

Waterproof matches and lighter: Starts a fire for safety, warmth, boiling drinking water, and cooking.

Whistle: Attracts attention if you are lost, stranded, or distressed.

Shelter: Tent for overnight hikes; space blanket for shorter hikes in case you become lost or injured.

Sightseeing: Camera and binoculars.

Now that you are fully prepared for your first hike let's dive straight into some of the most visited Southwest parks in the copper state of Arizona.

PART I
THE THREE NATIONAL PARKS OF ARIZONA

CHAPTER 2: GRAND CANYON NATIONAL PARK

"One of the world's most beloved attractions, Grand Canyon National Park never fails to dazzle its visitors. "The Grand Canyon fills me with awe. It is beyond comparison — beyond description; absolutely unparalleled throughout the wide world."

— THEODORE ROOSEVELT

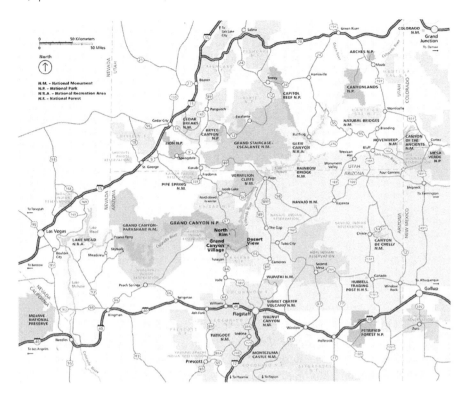

CONTACT INFORMATION

Website: *General Information*

Phone number: 928-638-7888

Address: 20 South Entrance Road, Grand Canyon, AZ 86023

PARK OVERVIEW

The Grand Canyon in northwest Arizona is one of the 7 natural wonders of the world and has been a UNESCO (United Nations Educational, Scientific and Cultural Organization) World Heritage Site since 1979. It has taken an astounding 6 million years for the Colorado River to etch away at the cliffs, creating peaks, buttes, gorges, and ravines.

There are 2 main park areas. The South Rim is 7,000 feet above sea level and is more popular due to greater accessibility. The North Rim sits 1,000 feet higher, and this higher elevation brings harsher weather and a shorter visitation season. There is also Grand Canyon West 4 hours from the South Rim. The Grand Canyon is popular for its expansive natural beauty and spectacular views of ancient rocks, cliffs, and mesas immersed in light and shadows. Along with tourists, it houses 100s of bird, reptile, fish, and mammal species that offer exhilarating encounters while hiking.

PLANNING

Local residents can swing by for the day to observe scenic overviews, take a short hike, and watch the sunset. If you traveled further and are seeking longer or more varied hikes and other activities, plan for 3 days.

Hotels at this popular park can be reserved up to 2 years in advance and typically sell out from March to October. Campground sites can be booked 6 months in advance.

Due to its vast size, Grand Canyon weather fluctuates drastically between an average temperature on the South Rim in January from 18–41°F and from 54–84°F in July. The North Rim can vary between 16–37°F in January and 46–77°F in July. It is warmest at the canyon bottom with January fluctuating between 36–56°F and July reaching temperatures of 78–106°F! There can be a temperature difference of 15–20°F between the top and bottom of the canyon. During winter, this difference may lead to the snow on both rims becoming rain by the time it reaches the bottom.

Grand Canyon is most crowded in July and August challenging a peaceful retreat. The weather is hot for hiking, and accommodations are more expensive. While the South Rim trails are open year-round, December to February hosts the fewest visitors. The North Rim area and services close from mid-October to mid-May because of the cold and snow.

Free Wi-Fi with limited bandwidth is available at the Canyon Village Market Deli, South Rim Yavapai Lodge, and North Rim General Camper store. Cell phone coverage is adequate within the South Rim especially around Grand Canyon Village. Coverage on the North Rim is often weak, and there is no signal at the bottom of the canyon at either rim. Both rims have a gas station and stores.

ADMISSION AND FEES

Fees & Passes

Free entry on 5 days; however, camping and tour fees still apply:

- Martin Luther King, Jr. Day (January)
- First Day of National Park Week (April)
- Anniversary of the Great American Outdoors Act (August)
- National Public Lands Day (September)
- Veterans Day (November)

Park admission (includes both rims) can be purchased with a credit/debit card (no cash) at all entrance stations or online and is valid for 7 days:

- Vehicle – Pass holder with up to 15 passengers = $35
- Motorcycle – Pass holder with 1 passenger = $30
- Pedestrian/Cyclist – Individuals on foot, bike, or park shuttle = $20 (under 16 years is free)
- *Digital passes*

Lifetime and annual passes are available at entrance stations, via phone 888-ASK-USGS or online at *entrance passes* (an additional $10 fee applies online):

- America the Beautiful Passes:

  - Annual Pass – General public for two individuals = $80
  - Military Annual Pass – Current U.S. military members and dependents = Free
  - Military Lifetime Pass – Gold Star Families and U.S. military veterans = Free
  - Senior Lifetime Pass – U.S. citizens and permanent residents 62 years old or over = $80 (provides additional discounts)
  - Senior Annual Pass – U.S. citizens and permanent residents 62 years old or over = $20
  - Access Pass – U.S. citizens or permanent residents with permanent disabilities = Free

(provides additional discounts)
  ○ Volunteer Pass – Those who have acquired 250 service
    hours on a cumulative basis = Free annually

- Every Kid Outdoors Annual 4th Grade Pass – 4th grade U.S.
  citizens and permanent residents = Free during the school year and
  subsequent summer
- Grand Canyon National Park Annual Pass – General public pass
  holder and vehicle guests or immediate family on foot, bike, or
  shuttle with unlimited visits to this park only = $70

America the Beautiful passes are honored at over 2,000 sites in the U.S.
managed by the Forest Service, National Park Service, Fish and Wildlife
Service, Bureau of Land Management, Bureau of Reclamation, and U.S.
Army Corps of Engineers.

DIRECTIONS

Flying:

- Phoenix, Arizona – *Phoenix Sky Harbor International Airport*
- Las Vegas, Nevada – *Harry Reid International Airport*

Driving:

- Rent a car from Phoenix airport and drive 232 miles (about 3.5
  hours) to the South Rim. Head to Williams (60 miles south of the
  park via Route 64 and U.S. 180) or to Flagstaff (80 miles southeast
  via U.S. 180 *or* U.S. 89 to Route 64 to the east entrance for *much less
  traffic*). Fill up your gas tank in one of these cities because gas
  stations are limited (and expensive!) closer to and inside the park.
- Rent a car from the Las Vegas airport and drive 277 miles (about 4
  hours) to the South Rim via U.S. 93 south and Interstate 40 (I-40)
  east.

Bus:

- Free National Park Shuttle Service – Service between Tusayan and Grand Canyon Village: *Grand Canyon park shuttle*
- Arizona Shuttle (now Groome Transportation) – Service from Phoenix airport, Sedona, and Flagstaff: *Groome Transportation*
- Grand Canyon Shuttle Service – Service from Phoenix and Flagstaff: *Grand Canyon shuttles*

Train:

- *Grand Canyon railway* operates between Williams, Arizona, and the South Rim
- *Amtrak* – Stations in Flagstaff and Kingman

ACCOMMODATIONS

Availability aside, seek accommodations that are close to everything you want to see:

Lodging – *Grand Canyon Village* has several lodges, most of which are within walking distance of the South Rim. Xanterra Parks and Resorts offers reservations for Bright Angel Lodge, El Tovar Hotel, Kachina Lodge, Thunderbird Lodge, Maswik Lodge, and Phantom Ranch. Phantom Ranch is the only lodging on the canyon floor and is accessible via mule ride, hike, or Colorado River rafting. *Delaware North* offers reservations for Yavapai Lodge and Trailer Village RV Park. Grand Canyon Lodge is the only *North Rim accommodation*.

Developed *Campgrounds*:

- South Rim Year-Round:

  - Mather – No hookups, laundry, showers, free shuttle bus service
  - Trailer Village RV – Full hookups, free shuttle bus

- South Rim Seasonal:

  - Desert View – Mid-April to mid-October, no hookups, 23 miles east of Grand Canyon Village
  - Ten-X – Mid-May to end of September, no hookups, 9 miles south of Grand Canyon Village

- North Rim Seasonal: mid-May to mid-October

  - North Rim – No hookups inside the park
  - Demotte – No hookups, 7 miles north of the park boundary

- Check to see if your campsite requires a _backcountry permit_

South Rim Pets:

- Leashed pets are allowed on trails above the rim, and at Mather/Desert View campgrounds, and Trailer Village RV park, as well as throughout developed areas where cars are allowed. Yavapai Lodge has pet friendly rooms. They are not allowed below the rim or on shuttle buses.
- _Grand Canyon kennels_

North Rim Pets:

- Allowed at Bridle and Arizona trail north of the park entrance station and Tuweep area (_North Rim pets_)

PARK ATTRACTIONS

- Park's cell phone tour number: 928-225-2907 to listen to Park Ranger audio tours at designated signs.
- Download the Grand Canyon app (GyPSy Guide app) for the _South Rim driving tour_.
- Bring a star chart or download a star app such as the _SkyView_® Free app for iPhone or Android to stargaze at the estimated 15,000 stars in the night sky.

- Biking: Bring your own or rent one from _Bright Angels bicycles_ next to the South Rim visitor center.
- Mule and horse rides: _Mule rides_ are offered from the South and North Rim. Horse trail rides are available from _Apache stables_. Check for age, clothing, height, weight, and weather restrictions for each ride.
- Drive from rim to rim: Travel 220 miles (5 hours) by car from rim to rim or take the _Trans-Canyon shuttle_.
- Whitewater rafting: _Wilderness River Adventures_ offers motor and oar powered rafting trips on the Colorado River and calmer river trips around Horseshoe Bend.
- Ride a _scenic train tour_ around the South Rim.
- Soar above the canyon on a _Papillon plane or helicopter ride_.

TOP HIKING TRAILS – LOCATIONS, SPECIFICATIONS, ACTIVITIES AND SITES

Beginner Trails – South Rim (With more Advanced Alternatives)

Rim Trail: Mather Point to Yavapai Point with Continuation to Canyon Village

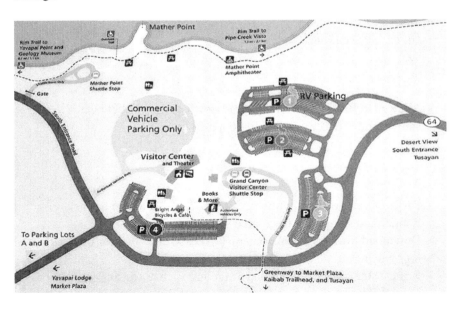

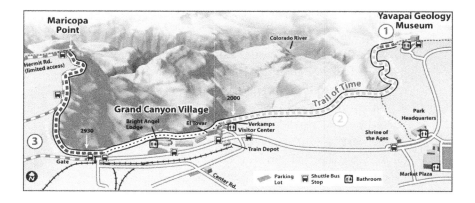

- Walk 0.3 miles from South Rim visitor center to Mather Point, which offers impressive views including O'Neill Butte, one of the most prominent features in the canyon.
- Continue 0.7 miles, 30 minutes, 82 feet elevation change to Yavapai Point and Yavapai Geology Museum with geology displays, ranger talks, souvenirs, water, and bathrooms. The enclosed glass observation deck offers awe–inspiring views a few thousand feet into the canyon to catch a glimpse of Phantom Ranch and the Colorado River.
- 1.3 mile "Trail of Time" geologic timeline pathway meanders from the museum to the historic _Grand Canyon Village_ with the lodges referenced earlier, Verkamp's Visitor Center, Railway Depot, Hopi House, Buckey O'Neill Cabin, Lookout Studio, and Kolb Studio, offering historical sites, restaurants, shops, water, and bathrooms.
- Mostly 5 feet wide paved asphalt to this point – wheelchair and stroller accessible, although help may be needed on some slight inclines.

  ○ Hike or ride the blue line _shuttle bus_ back that runs between the village and visitor center.
  ○ Or catch the red line shuttle bus that stops at each of the major viewpoints along Hermits Road, including Maricopa Point, with 180° views that are wheelchair and stroller accessible.

- *Advanced Alternatives Continue to:*

  - From the village, hike 7 miles along Hermit Road to Hermits Rest. Much of this route is not wheelchair or stroller accessible but offers stunning views of the Colorado River.
  - Hike the entire 13-mile South Rim trail from Hermits Rest in the west or South Kaibab trailhead in the east. Take the orange line shuttle from South Rim visitor center to South Kaibab trailhead.

Shoshone Point Trail

- Drive east on South Entrance drive from the visitor center to Desert View Drive. In 11 miles, stop off at Grandview Point, a 7,400–foot overlook with expansive views of ravines and cliffs around the Colorado River. Drive less than 2 miles more looking for a dirt parking lot with a gated road.
- 2.2 miles out-and-back, 265 feet elevation change, 45 minutes–1 hour.
- Dirt road 5 feet wide – wheelchair and stroller accessible.
- Toward the end of Shoshone path (slightly over a mile) are picnic tables, awnings for shades, and a toilet.
- Just past the picnic area a giant rock extends out that offers circular canyon views.
- Enjoy trail running, birdwatching, and snowshoeing in winter.

Beginner Trail – North Rim

Bright Angel Point Trail

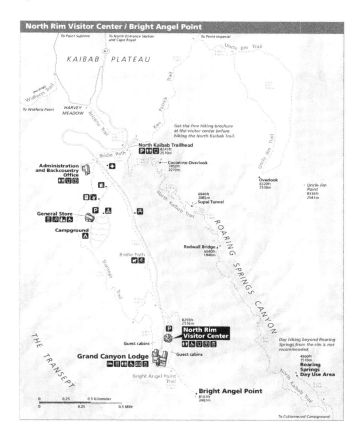

- Walk 0.25 miles from North Rim visitor center to Bright Angel Point.
- 0.5 miles out-and-back, 144 feet elevation change, 30 minutes.
- Mostly 3 feet wide paved asphalt with some bumps and cracks – partially wheelchair and stroller accessible with some steeper inclines and stairs. There are steep drops, so be careful along the edges.
- Offers beautiful sunrises and wildlife viewing opportunities.
- Bright Angel Point lookout gives views of Roaring Spring Canyon and Bright Angel Canyon.

Intermediate Trails (with Advanced Alternatives) – South Rim

After a short warmup and restock of snacks and water, it's time to consider trails that will exert you a little more in both distance and elevation. Remember, if you start to feel that a trail is too difficult, you can easily turn around and go back the way you came!

South Kaibab to Ooh Aah Point with Continuation to Cedar Ridge, Skeleton Point, Tip Off, and Phantom Ranch

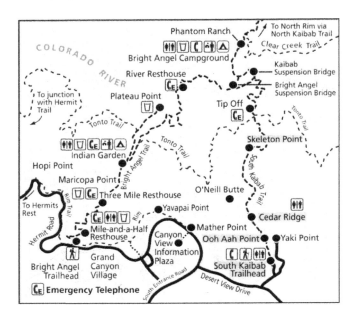

- Take the orange line shuttle from South Rim visitor center to South Kaibab trailhead or Yaki Point. Or take South Entrance Road to Desert View Drive and drive 1 mile to the Yaki Point access road. There's a parking lot just east of Yaki Road. The trailhead is south of Yaki Point on Yaki Point Road.
- 1.8 miles out-and-back, 790 feet elevation change, 1–1.5 hours to and from Ooh Aah Point.
- Well maintained dirt trail with switchbacks, meaning a sharp change in direction going up or down steep hills.
- Suitable for sturdy footed children but not wheelchairs or strollers.
- May be muddy, icy, and slippery in colder months requiring high traction boots and even walking sticks.

- Mules frequent this trail, so be prepared to step to the uphill side away from the edge.
- This is the only trail that follows a true ridgeline descent, which offers the unique opportunity to hike inside the canyon; however, this means exposure to weather elements, no water, and no bathrooms.
- Enjoy wildlife observation and wildflower identification.
- About 0.5 miles out Yaki Point will be on the right, and Ooh Aah Point is 0.4 miles further.
- Ooh Aah Point is so named because of its spectacular panoramic views of Pipe Creek Vista, O'Neill Butte, and Skeleton Point beyond that.
- Continue along the top of the ridgeline another 0.6 miles to Cedar Ridge with equally spectacular panoramic views.

  - 3 miles out-and-back to/from Cedar Ridge, 1,120 feet elevation change, 2–2.5 hours.
  - There are several narrow and steep switchbacks before Cedar Ridge.

- *Advanced Alternatives Continue to:*

  - Skeleton Point: 6 miles out-and-back, 2,040 feet elevation change, 4–6 hours.
  - Tip Off: 9 miles out-and-back, 3,280 feet elevation change, 6–9 hours.
  - Phantom Ranch: 15 miles out-and-back, 4,700 feet elevation change, 2 days.

    - Keep in mind that it can be dangerous to hike below Skeleton Point in one day, so an overnight stay is recommended before Tip Off.
    - An easier alternative is to take a *mule ride* to Phantom Ranch, although this books out far in advance.

Bright Angel Trail to 1.5 Mile Resthouse with Continuation to 3 mile Resthouse, Havasupai Garden (Formerly Indian Garden), Plateau Point, Bright Angel Campground, and Phantom Ranch

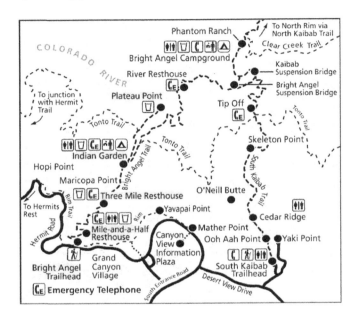

- Take the blue line shuttle from South Rim visitor center to Bright Angel Lodge. Or take South Entrance Road to Center Road and drive to the Grand Canyon Village where there are several parking lots. Trailhead is west of Bright Angel Lodge and Kolb Studio.
- 3 miles out-and-back to/from the first resthouse, 1,120 feet elevation change, 2–3 hours.
- Very popular, well maintained trail with some steep switchbacks.
- Suitable for sturdy footed children but not wheelchairs or strollers.
- Offers morning and afternoon shade. During winter months the ground can be icy necessitating high traction boots.
- Scrambling opportunity to use both hands and feet to climb.
- Rest on benches along the route.
- Enjoy beautiful views of canyon striations on the canyon walls.
- You will hit the first tunnel at 0.18 miles (0.36 miles out-and-back, 20–30 minutes) and the second tunnel at the 0.75-mile mark (1.5 miles out-and-back, 590–foot elevation change, 1–1.5 hours).

- At the 1.5-mile point, there is a resthouse with composting toilets, potable water (May–October), and an emergency phone.
- Continue another 1.5 miles to the 3 mile resthouse with composting toilets, potable water (May–October), and an emergency phone.

  ○ 6 miles out-and-back, 2,120 feet elevation change, 3–5 hours.

- *Advanced Alternatives Continue to:*

  ○ Havasupai Gardens: 9 miles out-and-back, 3,040–foot elevation change, 6–9 hours. You will find an oasis with cottonwood and elm trees and Havasu Creek.

    ◆ It can be dangerous to hike past Havasupai Gardens in one day, so an overnight stay is recommended at Havasupai Gardens campground or lodge. Here, you will find a ranger station, emergency phone, year–round potable water, picnic tables, and toilets.
    ◆ Visit Havasupai Falls and plunge pools by permit only.
    ◆ An easier alternative is to take a mule or helicopter ride to the bottom: *Havasupai falls*.

  ○ Plateau Point: 12 miles out-and-back, 3,080 feet elevation change, 9–12 hours. Enjoy sweeping views of the Colorado River.
  ○ Devil's Corkscrew (so named because of the heat in the summer) and then to Pipe Creek is another alternative. Beyond Pipe Creek are the River House rest area (8 miles from the trailhead), Bright Angel campground (9.5 miles from the trailhead), and Phantom Ranch (9.9 miles from the trailhead).

    ◆ You will discover beaches, sand dunes, a silver bridge over the Colorado River, fishing, and wildlife.

Advanced Trail – South to North Rims

Advanced trails combine distance with elevation and often take considerably longer; therefore, you can plan to do advanced trails over 2 days. Of all the trails in the Grand Canyon, the Rim to Rim trail is likely the most epic and adventurous.

Rim to Rim: North Kaibab to Grand Canyon Village

- North Kaibab trailhead is 41 miles south of Lake Jacob on Highway 67 (Hwy 67) with a small parking lot. Or park by Grand Canyon lodge and take the shuttle 1.5 miles north to the trailhead. North

Rim campground is 0.5 miles away. The Trans-Canyon shuttle also provides transportation between both rims.

- 22.8 miles rim to rim, 5,234 feet elevation change, 2–3 days.
- Stay at one of the campgrounds at the bottom – Bright Angel or Havasupai Gardens. Or, for a little luxury, stay at Phantom Ranch, one of America's most exclusive lodges, a Native American site full of history, cold beer, warm food, and comfy beds!
- From the trailhead, descend almost 6,000 feet to the bottom of the canyon. If you aren't up for the full descent, there are other scenic stopping points that offer shorter hikes:

  - Coconino Overlook: 1.3 miles out-and-back, 459 feet elevation change, 1 hour.
  - Supai Tunnel: 3.4 miles out-and-back, 1,377 feet elevation change, 2–3 hours with pit toilets and potable water (mid-May to mid-October).
  - Redwall Bridge: 5.2 miles out-and-back, 3,274 feet elevation change, 4–6 hours.

- Between the trailhead and Phantom Ranch, soak up the views of Ribbon Falls, Colorado River, huge rock formations, and all that nature has to offer.
- From the bottom of the canyon join the Bright Angel trail for the strenuous hike up to the South Rim.

The Rim to Rim trail is 1 reason to invest in an America the Beautiful Pass. So far, I have explored most parts of the Grand Canyon, but this trail is next on my bucket list! Now, let's head to our next park in Arizona.

CHAPTER 3: PETRIFIED FOREST NATIONAL PARK ARIZONA

"Quite a forest of petrified trees was discovered today...they were converted into beautiful specimens of variegated jasper. One trunk measured ten feet in diameter, and more than one hundred feet in length..."

— *LIEUTENANT AMIEL WEEKS WHIPPLE, 1853*

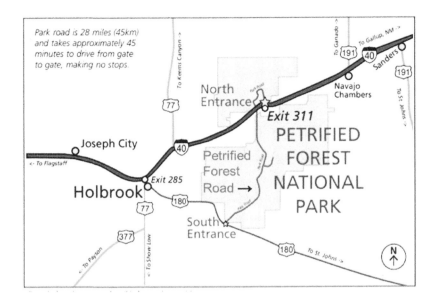

CONTACT INFORMATION

Website: *General Information*
Phone Number: 928-524-6228

Address: Petrified Forest National Park, P.O. Box 2217, AZ 86028

PARK OVERVIEW

The park's name comes from the world's largest and most colorful collection of petrified wood. When a tree falls, it either decomposes or undergoes permineralization in which some of the wood is fossilized and preserved to form petrified wood. Here, you will find the Chinle Formation, part of the Painted Desert, and 225-million-year-old fossils across historic structures and archeological sites. It's not all dry and arid land though, there are still several forest areas as the name suggests!

Petrified Forest is in eastern Arizona 19 miles east of Holbrook. The park has 2 areas, north and south, with separate entrances and visitor centers. The south part is larger and is joined to the north part by a narrow neck of land. In total, the park covers 346 square miles.

There are several reasons to visit this national park aside from the hikes. The wildlife is captivating with golden eagles flying overhead while coyotes and bobcats roam free. But it's the colors that will leave you speechless. Because of the minerals and metals absorbed by the wood it has transformed into bright hues of reds, browns, yellows, oranges, blues and purples.

PLANNING

Since this park is only a 3.5-hour drive from the Grand Canyon, you might want to consider adding a day to your trip to stop off here. 1 day is typically enough to see the main attractions and experience amazing hikes. Because this park is less busy, there is often no need to book in advance, which makes planning a little easier. The busiest times are spring and summer, but arriving early will help prevent you from getting stuck in traffic.

Petrified Forest National Park has extreme weather with hot summers, thunderstorms, and winter snow. It's not uncommon to have high winds. While spring and fall are good times to plan a trip, bear in mind that weather can be unpredictable in all seasons. Average temperatures in January range from 27°F– 48°F, whereas in July the difference can be from 40°F–90°F. August tends to be the wettest month.

Most of the park has cell coverage, but there may be a few dead zones around some of the larger land formations. Park rangers are available in case of emergency.

There is a diner and a convenience store within the park.

ADMISSIONS AND FEES

Fees & Passes

Petrified Forest offers the same 5 free days as Grand Canyon. Plus, America the Beautiful passes are accepted here. Aside from that, to enter the park, fees include:

- A vehicle with up to 15 passengers = $25
- Bikes and pedestrians = $15 per person (under 15 free)
- Motorcycles with 1–2 passengers = $20
- Annual Pass = $45

All passes are valid for 7 days and can be purchased at either of the entrances by credit or debit card or buy *entrance passes.*

DIRECTIONS

Flying:

- Phoenix, Arizona – *Phoenix Sky Harbor International Airport*
- Albuquerque, New Mexico – *Albuquerque International Sunport*

As there is no public transport, from here you will need to rent a car.

Driving:

- The park is 259 miles from the north and west sides of Phoenix or 215 miles from the east side.
- From Albuquerque it is a 204-mile drive.

Not all GPS systems will accurately take you to the park, so it's a good idea to notate the GPS coordinates given by the park: 35.06543746738773 (latitude) and 109.78153824806213 (longitude).

ACCOMMODATIONS

There are no lodges inside the park. With no formal campgrounds, camping is in the wilderness area at least half a mile from your vehicle. Obtain a free backpacking wilderness permit from the visitor center or Rainbow Forest Museum before 4:30 PM to spend the night in a tent. In order to protect the fragile soil and landscape, camping is limited to groups of 8 people and 4 horses: *eating & sleeping*.

Formal accommodations are available outside of the park including the rustic *Painted Desert ranger cabin*. There are also private *campgrounds* around the Navajo and Apache counties.

Petrified Forest is pet friendly allowing leashed companions on the trails just not inside buildings (see B.A.R.K. Ranger under Attractions).

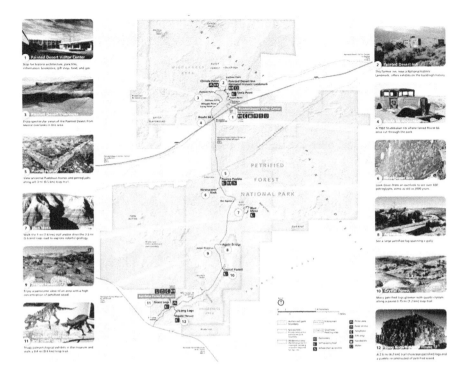

PARK ATTRACTIONS

- _B.A.R.K. Ranger_ Program: This is for your doggie family members who are allowed throughout the park but not inside buildings.
- Camping in Painted Desert: Discover wilderness stargazing experiences like no other using the _SkyView app_.
- _Rainbow Forest museum_: Has park information, backcountry permits, paleontological exhibits, movie, gift shop, snacks, and restrooms.
- Scenic Drive: 28.5-mile route from 1 entrance to the other between I-40 and I-180 where you can pull over to explore on foot or cycle.
- Route 66: This is the only national park that contains a portion of old _Route 66_. From the Painted Desert Inn, you will see a rusty old Studebaker car to mark what was once the country's most iconic road.
- Puerco Pueblo: These Puebloan house ruins may have homed up to 200 people between 1250 and 1380. The sandstone bricks outline over 100 rooms.

- Newspaper Rock: A little south of Puerco Pueblo sits this prehistoric rock possibly more than 2,000 years old with over 650 petroglyphs.
- *Cycling*: Bicycles and e–bikes are permitted on paved roads and parking lots.
- *Horseback riding*: 2 miles north of Painted Desert visitor center on the northwest side of Painted Desert Inn is the Painted Desert Wilderness access trail near Kachina Point where you will find trailer parking and room to load and unload.

TOP HIKING TRAILS – LOCATIONS, SPECIFICATIONS, ACTIVITIES AND SITES

Beginner Trails

Blue Mesa Trail

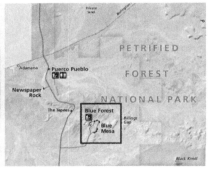

Walk the 1 mi (1.6 km) trail and/or drive the 3.5 mi (5.6 km) loop road to explore colorful geology.

- The trailhead is at the last parking lot on Blue Mesa Road.
- 1-mile loop, 114 feet elevation change, 20–30 minutes.
- Paved and gravel – suitable for children, but some steeper, zig-zagging turns into the valley are hard to navigate with wheelchairs or strollers.
- There is no shade.
- Read an informational bulletin board and plaques.
- Snack at the picnic pavilion.
- Observe striking color changes at sunrise and sunset.
- Admire the badlands in the valley with extensive erosion of various clay types exposing bands of blue, purple, gray, and peach.

- View the massive Triassic river system that is over 225 million years old.

Crystal Forest Trail

Many petrified logs glimmer with quartz crystals along a paved 0.75 mi (1.2 km) loop trail.

- The trailhead parking lot is 8 miles from the south entrance off Petrified Forest Road.
- 0.75-mile loop, 36 feet elevation change, 20–30 minutes.
- Paved with slight bumps and cracks – wheelchair and stroller accessible.
- Complete the loop clockwise or counterclockwise, but because of the low elevation there is little difference either way.
- Read informational plaques along the trail.
- There's a shade shelter that makes a lovely stop to enjoy some of the best views of petrified wood.

  - Conifers once grew here to over 200 feet, and after they were buried under volcanic ash crystals began to form inside the trees, so they now sparkle like gemstones.
  - You can exit the trail to examine each of the unique and massive logs.

Painted Desert Rim Trail

2 **Painted Desert Inn**

This former inn, now a National Historic
Landmark, offers exhibits on the building's history.

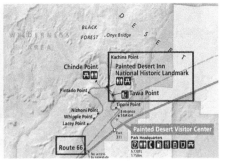

- The trailhead is at Tawa Point parking lot off Petrified Forest Road close to Route 66 and the rusted car.
- 1 mile out-and-back, 50 feet elevation change, 20–30 minutes.
- Dirt and gravel path that is easy to follow – suitable for children and seniors, but not wheelchairs or strollers.
- Follows the rim path heading northwest to Kachina Point where you can soak up the views and then head back on the same path.
- Since the earth is high in iron, there won't be much greenery unless it is right after a heavier rainfall.
- Look across at Pilot Rock, the tallest feature in the park standing over 6,000 feet.
- To extend your hike join the Onyx Bridge trail once you return to Tawa Point.

Giant Logs Trail

Study paleontological exhibits in the museum and walk a 0.4 mi (0.6 km) loop trail.

- The trailhead begins at Rainbow Forest Museum parking lot. Visit the museum before or after your hike.
- 0.4-mile loop, 36 feet elevation change, 15 minutes.
- Take the trail in either direction; there is also a smaller trail that heads straight through the middle.
- Paved with stairs – suitable for children but not wheelchairs or strollers.
- Enjoy an informational bulletin board and plaques, picnic pavilion, water bottle filling station, and bird watching.
- Witness some of the largest and most complete fossilized trees in the park dating between 219 and 213 million years old. "Old Faithful" is nearly 10 feet wide!
- The Mather Plaque (named after the first director of the National Park Service) is a short walk off the loop.
- Access the Long Logs and Agate House trails from the Rainbow Forest Museum.

Intermediate Trails

Historic Blue Forest Trail

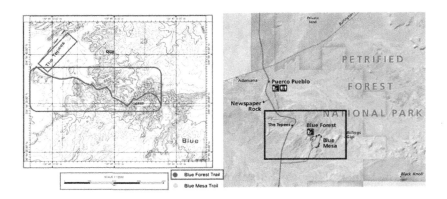

- The unmarked trailhead begins near The Teepees at a parking pullout.
- 2.5 miles out-and-back, 223 feet elevation change, 2–3 hours.
- Gravel and clay path that can be muddy and slippery when wet or icy. It can be windy too. Boots with good traction and a walking stick are recommended.
- Begins with switchbacks that gently incline to a wooden post that marks the end of the original 1937 road built by the Civilian Conservation Corp. Follow the gravel trails to the hoodoo rock formations keeping them on your right.
- Angle to the right following switchbacks to the top of the trail where you will find three small junipers. Turn around and head back to the trailhead.
- To extend the trail at the junipers veer off to the left where you can descend to the Blue Mesa trail.
- Aside from petrified logs, there are stunning views of the badlands along the hike.
- Marvel at the hoodoos, complex rock formations that are often wider at the top than the base.

Onyx Bridge Trail

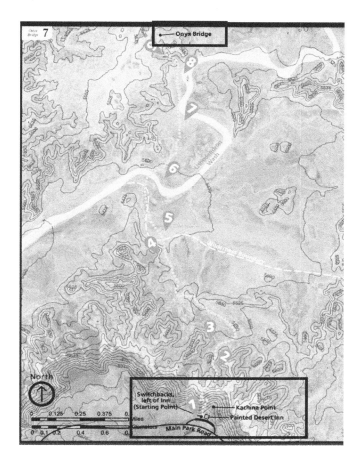

- The trailhead is at the Painted Desert Inn Museum parking lot. There are only natural markers on the trail, so it's worth getting a guide from the inn.
- 4 miles out-and-back, 300 feet elevation change, 3 hours.
- Gravelly and rocky with potential for loose pebbles.
- From the west of Painted Desert Inn, take steps to the switchback trail that descends into the valley where you will see red adobe hills.
- The next part of the trail consists of a series of washes (dried streams) that end at a rock fall (fallen, loose rocks) and Onyx Bridge.
- After snow melts and during monsoon season there may be water in the washes that will need to be traversed carefully.

- Onyx Bridge refers to a 30-foot-long fossilized log that is 210 million years old!
- On your way back to the inn you will see a long, petrified log that is visible because of soil erosion.
- Observe mesas, riverbeds, red deserts, and sometimes snow.
- There are quirky stone arrows, flowering cacti, and the chance to spot some reptiles.

Devil's Playground Loop

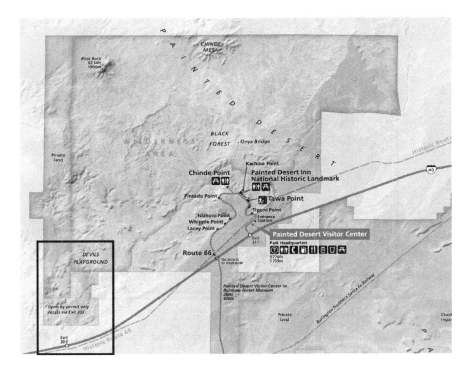

- The trailhead is accessible via exit 303 off 1–40 just west of the park's north entrance. There is a large open area for parking.
- 7.5-mile loop, 475 feet elevation change, 3 hours.
- Obtain a wilderness permit from the north entrance visitor center to hike Devil's Playground. Only 3 permits are issued per week on a first come first serve basis, so call ahead (928-524-6228) to inquire if a permit is available.
- The trail is marked by stakes.

- Enjoy wildlife, wildflowers, and bird watching.
- The hike to Devil's Playground takes you over Lithodendron Wash and follows other smaller washes to a mesa top.
- See Hoodoos Tower rock formation with bands of gray, purple, and blue.

Advanced Trails

Scenic Drive

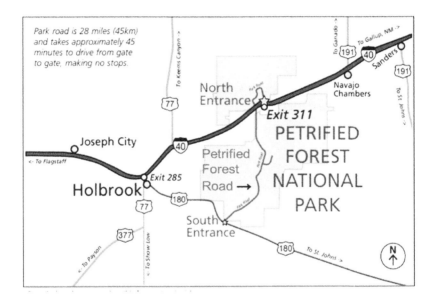

- Start at either park entrance, park your car, and arrange for someone to pick you up once you reach the other entrance.
- 28.4 miles point-to-point, 964 feet elevation change, 1–2 days.
- From the north end hike 5 miles along a mesa's edge offering breathtaking Painted Desert views.
- Cross I-40 and head south toward Puerco River through terrain covered with sagebrush, saltbrush, sunflowers, and Apache plume.
- After the river climb onto a narrow mesa that takes you to Newspaper Rock.
- The road twists southeast through a desolate stretch where you can catch a glimpse of tepee shaped buttes in the distance.

- Next you reach Blue Mesa at the park's midpoint with stunning petrified log views.
- Cross Agate Bridge, a 100-foot log over a wide wash.
- Jasper and Crystal Forest overlooks offer gleaming petrified wood views.
- Lastly, stop at Rainbow Forest museum for a rest!

* * *

As tempted as you may be to take home a souvenir it is strictly prohibited to remove petrified wood. Report anyone violating this rule to a park ranger. Take photos only as the history here goes much deeper than just a few fallen logs.

Our next national park takes us from giant wood to another giant feature that is symbolic of the Wild West!

CHAPTER 4: SAGUARO NATIONAL PARK

"Advice from a Saguaro, Stand tall, Reach for the sky, Be patient through the dry spells, Conserve your resources, Think long term, Wait for your time to bloom, Stay sharp!"

— *YOUR TRUE NATURE*

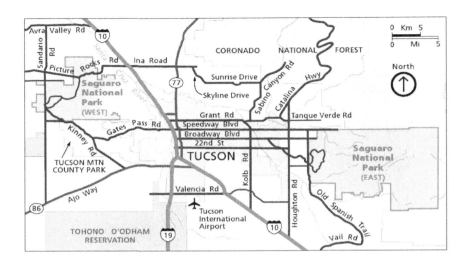

CONTACT INFORMATION

Website: *General Information*

Phone Number: 775-234-7331

Address: Tucson Mountain District, 2700 N. Kinney Road, Tucson, AZ 85743

PARK OVERVIEW

When you think of American West symbols from movies to cartoons, there is one image that stands out from the desert skyline, the giant cacti. Saguaro National Park protects some of the most amazing giant cacti or saguaros that can live for 200 years. Stand next to one of the 50-foot-tall plants to experience just how impressive they are.

Saguaro National Park offers more than a prickly view. As the most biodiverse desert in Northern America, you can take in pine and coniferous forests in the mountainous regions, and at just over 142 square miles, you are likely to spot an equally diverse range of animals. The park is home to 200 bird, 50 reptile, and 70 mammal species. You have everything from the desert tortoise to the black bear!

The park is separated into the east (Rincon Mountain District) and west (Tucson Mountain District) with the city of Tucson in the center. The park rests on Hohokam, O'odham, and Apache native lands, plus contains the Sonoran Desert, the only place where giant saguaros are native.

Inside the park, there are also the Saguaro National Park visitor center and the Arizona Sonora Desert Museum.

PLANNING

1–2 days is enough for this park. As with most parks, the best times to visit are spring and fall. While the summer months are most popular, the hot temperature can cause heat stroke as it's not unheard of to top 110ºF! This park is also popular in winter, but there might be some snow. The good news is that in winter you don't run the risk of meeting black bears on your hike! The average daytime winter temperature is 65ºF, dropping to 40ºF at night. Winter attracts more locals than large crowds.

Cell coverage is quite poor across the park, and there is no public Wi-Fi.

ADMISSIONS AND FEES

Fees & Passes

Similar to other national parks, you can enter the park for free on 5 days (Martin Luther King, Jr.'s birthday, the first day of National Park Week, the anniversary of the Great American Outdoors Act, National Public Lands Day, and Veterans Day). If you have an America the Beautiful pass, you can enter with this pass. Fourth graders can also enter for free with the Every Kid Outdoors pass. Those with a valid Interagency Pass can enter for free.

Other admission fees include:

- Vehicles with up to 15 passengers – $25
- Motorcycles – $20
- Annual Pass – $45

Purchase tickets at the east and west entrances by credit card. There is a self–pay option for when there is nobody at the gate. You can take an envelope and fill in your details; with this option, you can also pay with cash. Or purchase online at *entrance passes*.

DIRECTIONS

Flying:

Tucson, Arizona: *Tucson International Airport*

Driving:

From Tucson, take E. Valencia, then E. Irvington Road. It's approximately 25 minutes for the 15.7-mile drive. There are two entrances: Tucson Mountain District to the west (TMD) and the Rincon Mountain District to the east (RMD).

Bus:

You can hop on bus number 450 from Broadway/Houghton or number 7 from Golf Links/Kolb to get to the park: *Tucson buses*.

ACCOMMODATIONS

While reservations are not required to enter the park, a reservation and $8 permit are required for each campsite per night. Permits are available at *campgrounds and permits*. There is no RV park, and you can't drive vehicles to the campground, so you should plan this in your hike. There are 6 campsites:

- Manning Camp
- Spud Rock Spring
- Happy Valley Saddle
- Juniper Basin
- Grass Shack
- Douglas Spring

Each of the campgrounds has 3 sites, however, Manning Camp has 6. There is a limit of 18 people per group. Manning Camp also has a year-round supply of fresh water, although it should be treated first. For other sites bring the water you will need for your trip.

Pets are allowed at all campgrounds and picnic areas except for Mam-A-Gah. They are also allowed in parking areas/roads and the Desert Ecology/Desert Discovery trails on leash. Some of the trails permit horse-back riding.

There are also hotels in nearby Tucson including the *JTH Tucson* and *Choice hotels*.

PARK ATTRACTIONS

- Arizona *Sonora Desert museum*: Fun experience with a zoo, aquarium, botanical garden, and natural history display. 1.5 miles from the park's west side.
- Signal Hill Petroglyph: With over 200 prehistoric Native American petroglyphs estimated to be 550–1550 years old, this is the largest collection of its kind in the Tucson Mountain District. Although little is known about their meaning, these rock carvings are impressive. You can dine at the nearby Signal Hill Picnic Area.

- *Cactus garden*: This is a perfect place to start given its proximity to the *Red Hills visitor center*. A lovely, paved trail winds through towering cactus plants and chain fruit cholla, pencil cholla, and unique fishhook barrel cactus. Informational signs educate how the different plants have adapted to the area.
- Sunsets: Javelina Rocks, Signal Hill, and Gates Pass are some of the best locations to watch the sunset and take memorable photos of the cacti against the changing sky colors.
- *Cycling*: Bicycles and e-bikes are allowed throughout Tucson and the park. Biking around one of the scenic loop drives is a popular activity.

Saguaro West – Tucson Mountain District

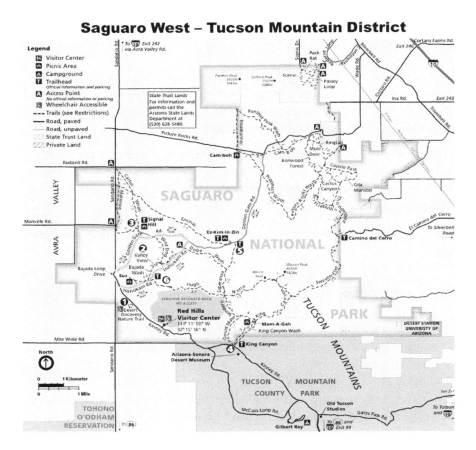

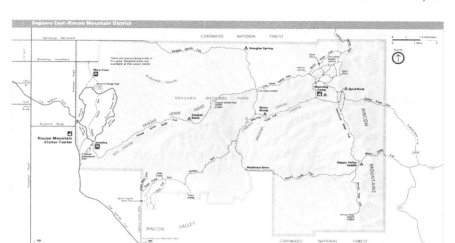

TOP HIKING TRAILS – LOCATIONS, SPECIFICATIONS, ACTIVITIES AND SITES

It's worth connecting some of the easiest trails to appreciate more of the park. The first trail is a perfect example.

Beginner Trails

Signal Hill Trail – West Side

- Park at the trailhead at the Signal Hill multiuse area off the unpaved Golden Gate Road.
- 0.5 miles out-and-back, 26 feet elevation change, 10 minutes.
- The trip out gradually inclines and climbs some rocky steps to the top of the hill.
- Trail running and horseback riding are welcome.
- Keep a look out for opuntia, cholla, and ocotillo cacti, as well as birds, wildlife, and informational plaques along the trail.
- The trail ends at Signal Hill picnic area with historical information and a wonderful viewpoint looking over the petroglyphs. There are toilets and even a grill!
- At the picnic area you will also find the trailhead for the Cactus Wren hike.

Desert Ecology Trail – East Side

- The trailhead is on Cactus Forest Loop Drive where there is parking.
- 0.5-mile loop, 10 feet elevation change, 10 minutes.
- Paved and 4 feet wide – wheelchair and stroller accessible.
- Travel north and then along Javelina Wash.
- There are a few benches along the way with many informational signs explaining the unique ecosystem in the area.
- Good for birdwatching, especially the Harris's hawk, elf owl, woodpecker, and quail.
- Aside from some truly massive cacti, you may see teddy bear cholla, prickly pear, barrel cacti, and chain fruit.

Mica View–Cactus Forest Loop Trail with Continuation to Cholla Trail – East Side

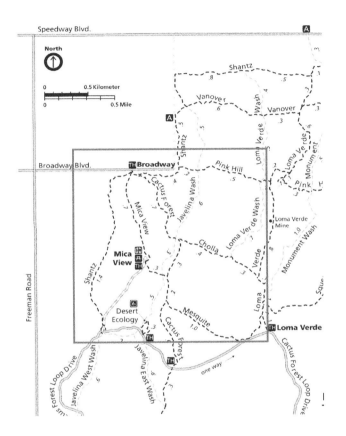

- The trailhead is off Cactus Forest Loop Drive with parking at the Mica View picnic area.
- 1.9-mile loop, 68 feet elevation change, 30–45 minutes.
- Start on the Mica View trail and continue to the right past Broadway trailhead and onto Shantz trail to join the Cactus Forest trail where you will cross 2 shallow washes followed by Javelina wash, and then curve back around to Mica View trail.
- Continue onto Cholla trail from Cactus Forest trail to complete a larger loop before getting back to Mica View.
- 3.8-mile loop, 124 feet elevation change, 1–1.5 hours.

- Popular for trail running and birdwatching, especially for Gila woodpeckers and Gilded flickers.
- Spot pencil, buckhorn, staghorn, and chain fruit cacti, as well as bushes, mesquite trees, and palo verde trees.
- Stunning views of Santa Catalina Mountains, Mica Mountain, and Tanque Verde Ridge.

Valley View Overlook Trail – West Side

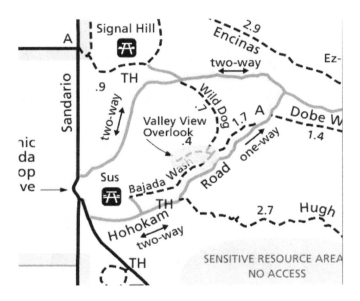

- The trailhead is north of Red Hills visitor center, just off Hohokam Road with parking to the left of this road.
- 0.8 miles out-and-back, 50 feet elevation change, 15–20 minutes.
- Packed sand – suitable for children and those walking with canes.
- Informational plaques along the way supply clues for plants and animals to search for so you can spot plants, wildlife, and different bird species.
- Soak up mountain and desert views, washes, and rolling hills.
- At the end of the trail are benches to rest and absorb the sights of Picacho Peak and Avra Valley. The valley reveals just how packed the park is with saguaros, like a scene from the movies.

Intermediate Trails

Bridal Wreath Falls Trail – East Side

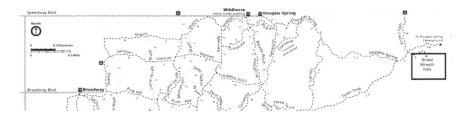

- The trailhead is off Douglas Spring trail at the east end of Speedway Boulevard where a paved parking lot offers more than 20 spaces.
- 5.7 miles out-and-back, 1,095 feet elevation change, 3 hours.
- Well maintained – suitable for older children.
- Starts off relatively flat and after crossing a creek you will reach Bridal Wreath Falls trail.
- 1 minute you are heading up through the mountains, and the next, you are in expansive grassy fields.
- After reaching Bridal Wreath Falls, return the way you came or extend the hike by joining the Three Tank trail.
- There are no bathrooms along this trail, so be sure to go beforehand and take plenty of water.
- Observe this rare desert waterfall and other waterfalls during the winter months.
- You may spot coyotes and deer along with various cacti species, palo verde trees, and desert shrubs.

Wasson Peak via King Canyon and Hugh Norris Trail – West Side

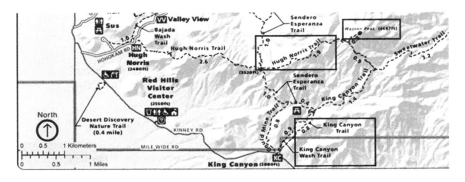

- The trailhead is at the King Canyon trailhead off N. Kinney Road where there is a parking area. Pass through a gate and picnic area.
- 7.9-mile loop, 1863 feet elevation change, 4 hours.
- Well maintained – suitable for older children.
- Gets a bit stony and steep as you head toward the top of the peak. There are slightly challenging switchbacks.
- After reaching the peak, head down some 900 feet on the Hugh Norris Trail with gentler switchbacks before returning to the King Canyon trailhead.
- While there are places to stop and rest, there are no bathrooms along the trail.
- Some spots may require scrambling with your hands on the ground because Wasson Peak is the tallest mountain in the Tucson Mountain District.
- From Wasson Peak, you have 360° views of the Tucson, Rincon, and Santa Catalina Mountain ranges.
- If you take this hike during spring, you will be rewarded with colorful, blooming cacti, as well as plenty of other wildflowers, dozens of lizards, and some rabbits.

Tanque Verde Ridge – East Side

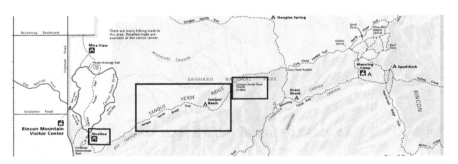

- The trailhead is at the Javelina picnic area where there is parking.
- 3.3 miles out-and-back, 925 feet elevation change, 2 hours.
- Starts with a moderate incline along the north ridge followed by a ravine below some small summits. It then climbs to the main ridge staying north of the crest.
- Though the route lacks signs, the trail is clear to follow.
- Extend the hike to Tanque Verde Peak.
- 17.6 miles out-and-back, 4,494 feet elevation change, 10 hours.

- Suitable for trail running, but there is no shade along the way.
- There is a bench to stop and rest.
- Spot colorful vegetation including jumping and teddy bear cholla, Arizona fishhook cacti, and hedgehog cacti as you head for the ridge. When you reach the ridge cacti will be replaced by yucca and agave.
- The ridge offers northern and southern views down to Box Canyon and Juniper Basin.

Gould Mine Loop – West

- The trailhead is at the King Canyon trailhead parking area.
- 2.3-mile loop, 380 feet elevation change, 1 hour.
- Rocky wide path – suitable for children.
- Clockwise around the loop is a gentler hike, but many feel the views are better going counterclockwise.
- Heading counterclockwise the trail begins quite flat until the first intersection. Keep left to the Mam-A-Gah picnic area and ascend gently up a ravine to the defunct copper mine with relics of tailing piles, 2 shafts, pieces of ironwork, and a stone cabin.
- Past the mine keep left to complete the loop.
- Connects to King Canyon trail to extend your hike.
- Observe wildlife including hawks, lizards, and coyotes. The saguaro provides shelter for owl nests, too.

- Eat at the Mam-A-Gah picnic area with views of King Canyon across the Avra Valley and over the Tucson Mountains.

Advanced Trails

<u>Wasson Peak via Sweetwater Trail – West Side</u>

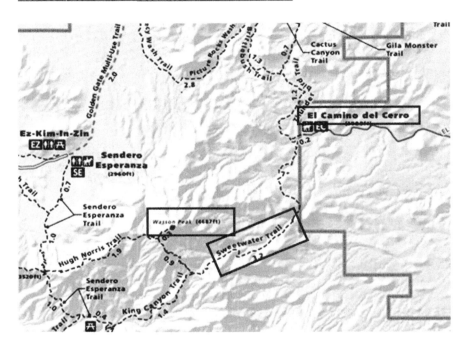

- Begin your hike by leaving the El Camino Del Cerro parking area and following the Sweetwater trail.
- 9.3 miles out-and-back, 2,093 feet elevation change, 5 hours.
- Rocky path – suitable for older children with some hiking experience.
- It's recommended to wear layers to protect against the heat and wind.
- This trail meets King Canyon trail where the path is then well signed to Wasson Peak. Traverse various switchbacks down into a canyon before a final push to the top of the peak.
- The views on the climb to over 4,000 feet high just get better and better including Safford and Panther Peaks.
- You will see teddy bear cacti, red barrels, cholla, and wildflowers.

- Sunset is ideal for this hike because of the light bouncing against the slopes of the Tucson Mountains.

Rincon Peak Trail – East Side

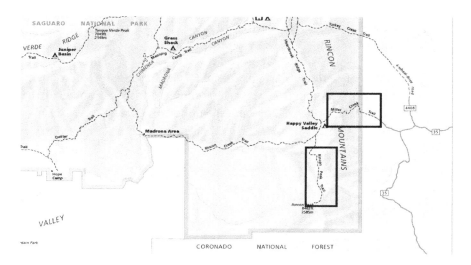

- Start on Miller Creek Trail off Route 35. There is a gate in the parking area that takes you straight onto Rincon Peak trail.
- 16.5 miles out-and-back, 4,200 feet elevation change, 6–8 hours.
- Begin by crisscrossing a creek with tall trees and a large field full of boulders before Happy Valley Saddle.
- While reaching the peak may seem daunting, it's only the last ½ mile that is really challenging at a 45º slope.
- You may need to scramble with your hands for support.
- It is one of the least visited sites with an average of 1 visitor per day, so it is ideal if you are hoping for some solitude.
- Diverse terrain including a creek, large trees offering some shade, colorful wildflowers, and an abundance of cacti species.
- Rincon Peak is the second highest in the park. It consists of solid stone with little vegetation, but the 360º views are well worth the final push. Some compare the views to looking out of an airplane window.

Saguaro National Park is the perfect place to experience various ecosystems in 1 place. Some of the shorter hikes are incredibly popular, but others are really isolated. Compared with other parks, there are also few facilities along the trails. Take advantage of parking areas for bathroom stops and water, and always be prepared for rapid changes in the weather.

* * *

Our next series of national parks takes us to California, and while many head to the touristy spots of L.A., we are going to discover some of the natural secrets of the Golden State right next door to Arizona.

PART II
THE NINE NATIONAL PARKS OF CALIFORNIA

CHAPTER 5: CHANNEL ISLANDS NATIONAL PARK

"Man cannot discover new oceans unless he has the courage to lose sight of the shore."

— *ANDRE GIDE*

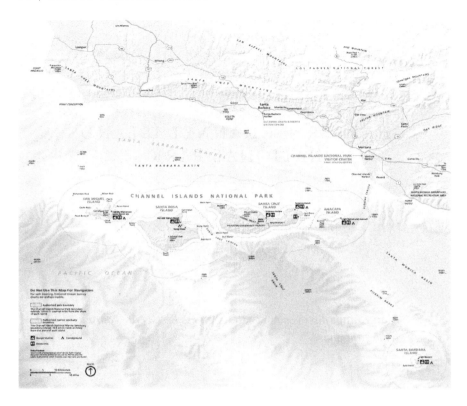

CONTACT INFORMATION

Website: *General Information*

Phone Number: 805-658-5730

Address: 1901 Spinnaker Drive, Ventura, CA 93001

PARK OVERVIEW

Established as a national park in 1980, the park consists of 5 islands: Anacapa, Santa Cruz, Santa Rosa, San Miguel, and Santa Barbara.

Channel Islands National Park is aptly nicknamed the "Galapagos of North America" because it hosts such diverse species. The islands are home to 2,000 plant and animal species, 145 of which can't be found anywhere else on the planet such as the island fox, island deer mouse, and spotted skunk.

An impressive 10% of the world's blue whale population gathers off the islands during summer, and there are opportunities to see them other times of the year too.

For a trip into the unknown, explore Painted Cave, a massive cavern that covers the length of 4 football fields with a soaring entrance of 160 feet. Above ground, you can spot some of the most unique pine trees in the world. Santa Rosa Island is home to the Torrey pine tree, one of only two places where this species grows naturally.

Channel Islands offers unspoiled hikes and a complete escape to nature.

PLANNING

While there are hikes that only require a day, it is well worth planning 2–3 days to fully appreciate the experience. This is 1 national park where careful planning is required because there are no services or shops on the island you need to pack everything for your stay before you leave, including water! The only structures you will find are various visitor centers/ranger stations: Robert J. Lagomarsino visitor center, Outdoors Santa Barbara visitor center, Santa Barbara Island visitor center, Anacapa Island visitor center, Scorpion Ranch visitor center on Santa Cruz Island, Santa Rosa Island visitor contact station, and San Miguel Island ranger and visitor contact station: *visitor centers and ranger stations*.

The only way to stay on the islands is camping by making reservations up to 6 months in advance and showing proof of reservation upon arrival.

The Mediterranean climate also makes the islands highly appealing with temperatures ranging from the low 50s–low 70s°F in summer. However, these islands can experience 4 seasons in 1 day. Come prepared for sea spray, fog, and high winds. The best season to visit is often early fall because winds are calmer and visibility is better. In terms of crowds, it's one of the least visited national parks in the U.S. with less than 500,000 annual visitors.

There is no Wi-Fi on the islands and cell service is sketchy unless you are on the mainland or the visitor center in Ventura. In case of emergency you will need to locate staff at the park.

ADMISSION AND FEES

Fees & Passes

Channel Islands National Park is even more appealing with no admission fees; however, remember that traveling to and activities on the islands will require payment.

DIRECTIONS

It is likely that you will need various forms of transport to reach the islands.

Flying:

Los Angeles, California: *Los Angeles (LAX) Airport*

Driving:

Rent a car at the airport and drive to either Ventura or Santa Barbara, both southeast of L.A.

- Ventura – follow I-405 N, CA-118 W, and U.S. 101 N for a total of 66 miles.
- Santa Barbara – 96-mile drive along the U.S. 101 N.

Boat:

Island Packers runs boats from Ventura and Santa Barbara on various days and times to the different islands for various fees as outlined on their website.

- Inner Islands: Approximately 1-hour trip to Anacapa and Santa Cruz. Boat rides are available year-round. Visitors must be prepared to climb stairs and ladders upon arrival. Trips that don't go ashore are available to view wildlife, including seasonal whale watching excursions.
- Outer Islands: Approximately a 3–4-hour trip to Santa Rosa, San Miguel, and Santa Barbara. Boat rides are available from March–November. Santa Rosa and Santa Barbara have stairs/ladders to climb upon arrival. Landing for San Miguel is via skiffing onto the beach, so visitors should have waterproof gear and

prepare to get wet among wind and rough waters. At the time of publication, Santa Barbara is closed due to dock damage.

ACCOMMODATIONS

Ventura and Santa Barbara have restaurants and accommodations, but there is only primitive camping on each of the islands. To make a reservation, call 877-444-6777 or visit *campground reservations*.

- Santa Barbara – Landing Cove
- Anacapa – On the East Islet
- Santa Cruz – Scorpion Ranch
- Santa Rosa – Water Canyon
- San Miguel – Above Cuyler Harbor

Camping costs $15 per night. All equipment must be carried to the campsites as there is no transport on the islands. Secure food in boxes/coolers otherwise wildlife may help themselves to your meals. Remove all your trash as there are no trash containers. Fires aren't permitted, but enclosed gas camp stoves are: *campground information.*

No pets are allowed on any of the islands.

PARK ATTRACTIONS

- There are a range of *activities* including boating, kayaking, scuba diving, snorkeling, fishing, surfing, whale watching, and bird watching on the various islands.
- Anacapa Island: This island is famous for its three islets, almost 5 miles long, where waves have eroded the volcanic island creating sea cliffs, caves, and natural bridges. The west cliffs house the largest breeding colony of endangered California brown pelicans. All the islets are home to the world's largest breeding colony of western gulls.
- Santa Cruz Island: Here you will find sweeping views of Potato Harbor and Scorpion Canyon with wildlife, including whales, dolphins, foxes, and dozens of bird species.
- Santa Rosa Island: Enjoy the white sand of Water Canyon Beach and have a picnic. Hiking across the island will allow you to see a host of wildlife, rolling hills, and the stunning Lobo Canyon.
- Channel Islands National Marine Sanctuary: 1,470 square miles of ocean is home to endangered species, historic shipwrecks, and a hub for research, education, and conservation. Visitors can see seabirds, whales, dolphins, sharks, seals, and sea lions while partaking in boating, diving, and kayaking. Visit the office in the Ocean Science Education Building in Santa Barbara, call 805-699-5422, or visit their website *marine sanctuary*.
- Sea Caves: It is well worth joining one of the professional boating or kayaking tours to fully appreciate the sea caves and diverse wildlife while learning a wealth of knowledge from the friendly guides. Go through Island Packers to book island tours, kayak tours, educational tours, harbor cruises, and overnight camping trips: *kayaking, tours, and cruises.*

TOP HIKING TRAILS – LOCATIONS, SPECIFICATIONS, ACTIVITIES AND SITES

Beginner Trails

<u>Potato Harbor – Santa Cruz Island</u>

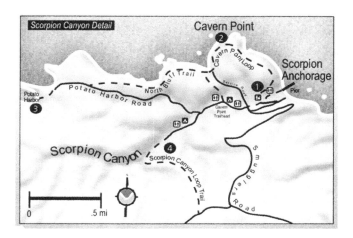

Destination	Distance (miles, round-trip)	Difficulty	Description
From Scorpion Beach:			
① Historic Ranch	5	Easy	View the historic Scorpion Ranch complex dating to the late 1800s. Exhibit areas include an orientation kiosk, blacksmith shop, farm implements, and a visitor center located in the Scorpion ranch house
② Cavern Point Loop	2	Moderate	Not to be missed. Magnificent coastal vistas and seasonal whale viewing. To avoid a steep climb, hike clockwise, beginning from campground (near site #22) and looping back to Scorpion Anchorage. From Cavern Point, you may also follow the North Bluff Trail west for 2 miles out to Potato Harbor
③ Potato Harbor	5	Moderate	A longer hike than the Cavern Point hike, but also with spectacular coastal views. No beach access
④ Scorpion Canyon Loop	4.5	Moderate to strenuous	A scenic loop hike to the interior with a chance to see the unique island scrub-jay. To avoid a steep climb, hike clockwise starting on the Smugglers Road towards the oil well and eventually down into Scorpion Canyon and back out to the beach. Hike off trail into the right (or northwest) fork of Scorpion Canyon to see the island scrub-jay, but be prepared for extremely rocky conditions

- The trailhead is at Scorpion Anchorage.
- 5 miles out-and-back, 600 feet elevation change, 2–2.25 hours.
- Suitable for children.
- Well signed from Cavern Point loop to Northern Bluff trail and then on to Potato Harbor.
- Potato Harbor is named after its shape. There is no access to the beach due to steep cliffs.
- Bring binoculars to spot wildlife, in particular puffins and other bird species.

- Notice the bright white sedimentary rock known as diatomaceous earth, which is created from tiny single cell sea plants called diatoms.
- Looking down over Potato Harbor you may see a giant kelp forest and even sea lions.
- Relatively flat terrain is suitable for trail running, although care should be taken on rocky parts.

Cavern Point Loop – Santa Cruz Island

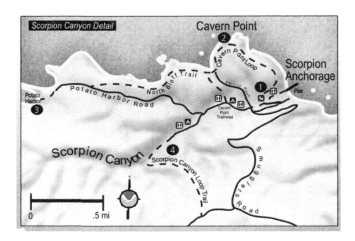

Destination	Distance (miles, round-trip)	Difficulty	Description
From Scorpion Beach:			
1 Historic Ranch	5	Easy	View the historic Scorpion Ranch complex dating to the late 1800s. Exhibit areas include an orientation kiosk, blacksmith shop, farm implements, and a visitor center located in the Scorpion ranch house.
2 Cavern Point Loop	2	Moderate	Not to be missed. Magnificent coastal vistas and seasonal whale viewing. To avoid a steep climb, hike clockwise, beginning from campground (near site #22) and looping back to Scorpion Anchorage. From Cavern Point, you may also follow the North Bluff Trail west for 2 miles out to Potato Harbor.
3 Potato Harbor	5	Moderate	A longer hike than the Cavern Point hike, but also with spectacular coastal views. No beach access.
4 Scorpion Canyon Loop	4.5	Moderate to strenuous	A scenic loop hike to the interior with a chance to see the unique island scrub-jay. To avoid a steep climb, hike clockwise starting on the Smugglers Road towards the oil well and eventually down into Scorpion Canyon and back out to the beach. Hike off trail into the right (or northwest) fork of Scorpion Canyon to see the island scrub-jay, but be prepared for extremely rocky conditions.

- The trailhead is at Scorpion Anchorage.
- 2 miles out-and-back, 292 feet elevation change, 45–60 minutes.
- Some steep parts, but suitable for children.
- After 0.35 miles, you will have ascended the steepest incline where you will see endless views of Point Conception to the Ventura coastline.

- Head west toward Scorpion Ranch campground with a rocky descent, so be careful if you return after sunset.
- The views are the main attraction of this hike. Toward the east you will see Anacapa, and on a clear day you can spot California's coastline.
- Though you can't see it, you will be walking over the island's largest sea caves!

East Anacapa Island Trail – East Anacapa Island

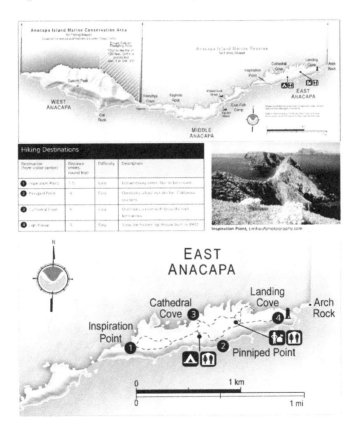

Inspiration Point, timhaufphotography.com

- The trailhead is at Landing Cove.
- 2.5-mile loop, 400 feet elevation change, 1–1.25 hours.
- Suitable for children.
- At the beginning of the trail is the huge Fresnel lens at the visitor's center, which used to occupy the top of the lighthouse.

- Head east to the lighthouse where you will see the 40-foot-high Arch Rock.
- Then head back southwest toward Pinniped Point around to Inspiration Point, Cathedral Cove, and back to Landing Cove.
- At Pinniped Point keep an eye out for pelagic birds, sea lions, dolphins, and whales.
- Inspiration Point yields epic views of the middle and west Anacapa Islands, Santa Cruz, San Miguel, and the rest of Channel Islands.
- Cathedral Cove has abundant gulls and pelicans. If you hike in spring, you may even see nests with chicks.

Intermediate Trails

Smuggler's Cove – Santa Cruz Island

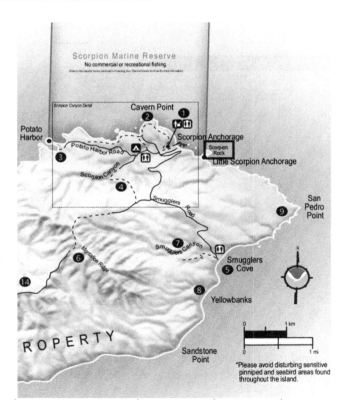

⑤ Smugglers Cove	7.5	Strenuous	Follow the Smugglers Road to the beach at Smugglers Cove. Carry water. No water available at Smugglers.	
⑥ Montañon Ridge Loop	10	Strenuous	Great views, for experienced hikers only. Trail not maintained. Carry a topographic map. This loop can be accessed via Smugglers Road or via the North Bluff Trail near Potato Harbor.	
From Smugglers Cove:				
⑦ Smugglers Canyon	2	Strenuous	Off-trail hiking in a stream bed (seasonal water) with steep canyon walls. Uneven terrain and loose rock.	

- The trailhead begins just after the sign for the Cavern Point trail.
- 7.7 miles out-and-back, 1,414 feet elevation change, 4–5 hours.
- After stopping at Scorpion Rock to take in the views, head inland passing Cypress Tree Grove.
- The trail splits toward the oil well or Smuggler's Cove. Follow the oil well trail, which offers a nice break as it is flat for a mile and reveals stunning views of Anacapa. The next mile is a steep descent into Smuggler's Cove. Watch your footing on the path to the beach as it can be rocky.
- Rather than passing Cypress Tree Grove, take the short trail to explore them closer and enjoy a shaded picnic.
- The beach at Smuggler's Cove contains animal bones and other remnants of the clandestine traders (smugglers) from Spanish colonial times.
- About 0.2 miles from the beach is a partially restored ranch.
- Though the historic oil well struck water you can still see traces of the old pipeline along the trail.
- In the wet seasons there are some beautiful cascades.
- The beach has a pit toilet and benches.

Scorpion Canyon Loop Trail – Santa Cruz Island

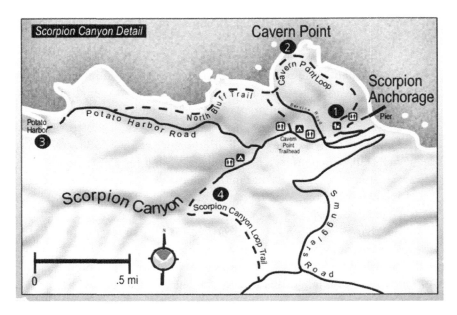

Destination	Distance (miles, round-trip)	Difficulty	Description
From Scorpion Beach:			
① **Historic Ranch**	5	Easy	View the historic Scorpion Ranch complex dating to the late 1800s. Exhibit areas include an orientation kiosk, blacksmith shop, farm implements, and a visitor center located in the Scorpion ranch house.
② **Cavern Point Loop**	2	Moderate	Not to be missed. Magnificent coastal vistas and seasonal whale viewing. To avoid a steep climb, hike clockwise, beginning from campground (near site #22) and looping back to Scorpion Anchorage. From Cavern Point, you may also follow the North Bluff Trail west for 2 miles out to Potato Harbor.
③ **Potato Harbor**	5	Moderate	A longer hike than the Cavern Point hike, but also with spectacular coastal views. No beach access.
④ **Scorpion Canyon Loop**	4.5	Moderate to strenuous	A scenic loop hike to the interior with a chance to see the unique island scrub-jay. To avoid a steep climb, hike clockwise starting on the Smugglers Road towards the oil well and eventually down into Scorpion Canyon and back out to the beach. Hike off trail into the right (or northwest) fork of Scorpion Canyon to see the island scrub-jay, but be prepared for extremely rocky conditions.

- The trailhead is just past the Scorpion Ranch campground.
- 4.1-mile loop, 770 feet elevation change, 2–2.25 hours.
- Taking the trail counterclockwise is easier on the legs.
- Head south on Smuggler's Road, which begins to incline.
- At the 1.7-mile mark, the trail splits. Keep to the right toward Scorpion Canyon loop.
- From the plateau the trail takes a right turn into one of the steepest declines of the loop before leveling off until mile 2.9 where you will start to descend to the campground.
- At mile 2.1 you can exit the trail to see the aforementioned oil well.

- Smuggler's Cove and Scorpion loop can be combined for a longer hike.
- Some parts of the trail are relatively flat making it suitable for trail running.
- Identify native island plants.

Pelican Bay – Santa Cruz Island

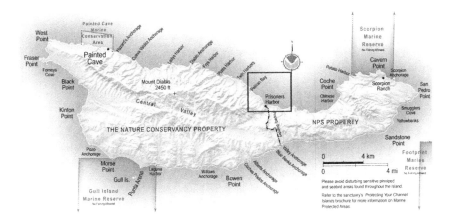

- The trailhead begins at Prisoners Harbor on the Northwest shore of the island.

  - Hikers must be accompanied by Island Packers staff, or private boaters must obtain a landing permit.

- 3.9 miles out-and-back, 820 feet elevation change, 2–2.25 hours.
- Fairly rugged with some steep hillsides.
- The first viewpoint after an uphill hike is a historical cabin used around a century ago. It was rented out to recreational hunters and fishermen by Ira Eaton who leased Pelican Bay from the Santa Cruz Island Company from 1910–1937.
- After various ups and downs and some interesting-shaped trees, the trail reveals the first view of Pelican Bay.

  - From here you can either turn around or carry on to a slightly more difficult stretch with steeper drops and poison ivy patches.

- Ends with never ending views of Pelican Bay ahead and Prisoners Harbor behind.
- This trail spans Nature Conservancy property making it ideal for enjoying nature and wildlife because it is protected. Look out for scrub jays and the Santa Cruz Island fox. Looking across the water you may see seals, sea lions, and dolphins.

Advanced Trails

Montañon Ridge Loop – Santa Cruz Island

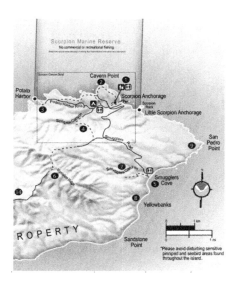

	Smugglers Cove	7 5	Strenuous	Follow the Smugglers Road to the beach at Smugglers Cove. Carry water. No water available at Smugglers
	Montañon Ridge Loop	10	Strenuous	Great views, for experienced hikers only. Trail not maintained. Carry a topographic map. This loop can be accessed via Smugglers Road or via the North Bluff Trail near Potato Harbor
From Smugglers Cove:				
	Smugglers Canyon	2	Strenuous	Off-trail hiking in a stream bed (seasonal water) with steep canyon walls. Uneven terrain and loose rock

- The trailhead is accessible from North Bluff Trail near Potato Harbor or via Smuggler's Road.
- 8.8-mile loop, 1,699 feet elevation change, 4.5 hours.
- Take a paper map because the Montañon Ridge part of the trail is not well maintained.

- Starts uphill and becomes rocky in places. Mile point 3.5 is the first viewpoint where you can appreciate the size of Santa Cruz, and a little further on, Prisoner's Harbor.
- The next part veers southeast with some steep descents toward Scorpion Anchorage with a view of Anacapa.
- Much of the trail at the highest points follows the backbone of the ridge, so be careful.
- The ridge can be followed back down to Potato Harbor.
- The views are by far the highlight of this trail. Montañon Ridge marks the highest elevation on eastern Santa Cruz and is the tallest accessible peak in the entire national park.
- Diverse terrain offers the chance to see seals and dolphins as well as island foxes in the lower altitudes, along with coastal shrubs, open prairies, and oak woodland.

Del Norte Trail and Navy Road Loop – Santa Cruz Island

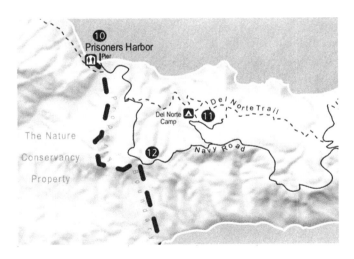

From Prisoners Harbor:

⑩ Prisoners Harbor	5	Easy	Walk through the ranch area, wetland and up the Navy Road for a short distance to get a nice harbor view.
⑪ Del Norte Overlook	3	Moderate	Hike 1 mile up the Navy Road to the Del Norte Trail junction and then follow the trail for 2.5 miles to an overlook of the northwest coast.
⑫ Del Norte Camp	3	Strenuous	Follow the rugged Del Norte trail east to the backcountry camp. Carry water. No water at this campground.
⑬ Del Norte / Navy Road Loop	8.5	Strenuous	This loop provides views to the south side of the island. Follow the Del Norte Trail to the Del Norte Road that leads south to the campground. Continue south on this road to the Navy Road and return to Prisoners.

Omitted from map

#11

#12

- The trailhead is at Prisoner's Harbor starting on Navy Road.
- 8.01-mile lollipop loop, 1,807 feet elevation change, 4–4.25 hours.
- Hike 1 mile to the Del Norte trail junction and follow Del Norte trail 0.25 miles to the Del Norte overlook. Continue east to Del Norte campground (3.5 miles from the trailhead).
- From the campground, the loop links back onto Navy Road and back to Prisoner's Harbor.
- The trail can get a little muddy in the wet months.
- Some parts of the trail are suitable for trail running.
- Travels through oak woodlands with stunning views of Santa Barbara Channel, Prisoner's Harbor, and the Santa Cruz Island coastline.
- Picnic table and pit toilet available.
- Primitive camping: 4 sites each for 4 people. For camping, bring everything you will need, including toilet paper! Double check availability and reserve at _Santa Cruz Del Norte backcountry_.

2 things must be emphasized when visiting the Channel Islands. First, be fully prepared. Potable water and shade are scarce; therefore, pack extra water and sun protection. Second, the only way off the islands is by boat. Boats tend to depart promptly and don't hang around until everyone has returned to the dock, meaning if you aren't back in time, you risk being stranded on 1 of the islands with no facilities! Always keep an eye on the time as you are hiking.

* * *

The next park in California sounds far scarier than it really is!

CHAPTER 6: DEATH VALLEY NATIONAL PARK

"*Amidst the desolation of Death Valley, I find a sense of peace and solitude.*"

— *UNKNOWN*

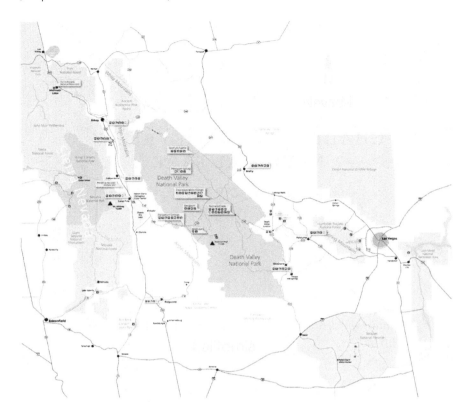

CONTACT INFORMATION

Website: _General Information_

Phone Number: 760-786-3200

Address: P.O. Box 579 Death Valley, CA 92328

PARK OVERVIEW

This is America's lowest, hottest, driest national park, holding the world record for the hottest temperature of 134°F in 1913 (_National Park Service_, n.d.). Legend has it that the area got its name in 1849 during the gold rush when one of the 49 gold seeking pioneer prospectors thought the valley was a shortcut to his wealth. His last words were supposedly "Goodbye, Death Valley." Despite this, the desert set between snow-capped mountains is now alive with activity.

Death Valley was named a national monument in 1933 and a national park in 1994. The park covers 5,270 square miles making it the 5th largest national park in the U.S. It is also an International Dark Sky Park with amazing opportunities for stargazing.

This park is home to 51 mammal, 300 bird, and 36 reptile species. Surprisingly, there are also over 1,000 types of plants, and 23 of those are unique to Death Valley. The range of elevations is also impressive. Hikes can take you past salt flats, sand dunes, mountains, badlands, and canyons. Death Valley is also steeped in gold, silver, copper, tungsten, lead, and zinc mining.

PLANNING

While you can complete many hikes in 1 day, 2 days is ideal to appreciate more of the national park due to its large size. There are several camp-grounds, most of which work on a first-come-first-serve basis, so advanced booking isn't necessary except for free park days.

The weather is the biggest consideration for planning. Summer is often too hot as April–October temperatures can reach upward of 100°F. Early spring is the best time to visit to see flowers that burst into life and to participate in the Death Valley Dark Sky Festival. However, late fall is perfect for clear skies, slightly cooler temperatures, and avoiding crowds.

Cell phone service is sporadic. Your phone may work in areas such as Furnace Creek and Stovepipe Wells, but it will be slower, and you might need to switch your settings to roaming. Wi-Fi is available at the Death Valley Lodging Company in Stovepipe Wells, but again, it's limited. Wi-Fi can also be purchased from The Oasis at Death Valley in Furnace Creek.

ADMISSION AND FEES

Fees & Passes

Many of the passes are the same as for other national parks, such as the America the Beautiful Annual Pass, 4th Grade Pass, Annual Pass for US Military, Lifetime Pass for Veterans and Gold Star Families, and Access Pass for those with disabilities.

Other fees include:

- Vehicles – $30
- Motorcycle – $25
- Individuals – $15
- Annual Pass – $55
- Annual Senior Pass – $20
- Lifetime Senior Pass – $80

You can pay at any of the park entrances by credit card.

DIRECTIONS

Flying:

- Las Vegas, Nevada – *Harry Reid International Airport*

Driving:

There is no public transport or shuttle buses to Death Valley. Rent a car from Las Vegas airport and drive approximately 2 hours to the park. From the east side, you can enter via:

- CA 190 from Death Valley Junction, CA
- SR 374 from Beatty, NV
- CA 178 from Shoshone, CA

From the west side, you can enter via:

- CA 190 from Olancha, CA
- SR 178 (Panamint Valley Rd), CA

As there is no specific address, GPS may send you down dead-end or closed roads. The Furnace Creek Visitor Center coordinates are N36°27.70, W 116°52.00.

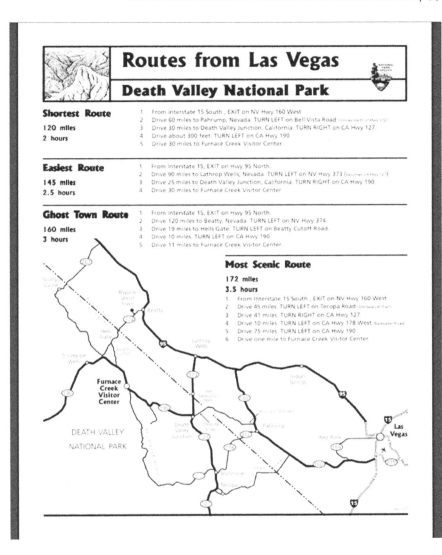

Routes from Las Vegas
Death Valley National Park

Shortest Route

120 miles

2 hours

1 From Interstate 15 South , EXIT on NV Hwy 160 West
2 Drive 60 miles to Pahrump, Nevada. TURN LEFT on Bell Vista Road
3 Drive 30 miles to Death Valley Junction, California. TURN RIGHT on CA Hwy 127
4 Drive about 300 feet. TURN LEFT on CA Hwy 190.
5 Drive 30 miles to Furnace Creek Visitor Center.

Easiest Route

145 miles

2.5 hours

1 From Interstate 15, EXIT on Hwy 95 North.
2 Drive 90 miles to Lathrop Wells, Nevada. TURN LEFT on NV Hwy 373
3 Drive 25 miles to Death Valley Junction, California. TURN RIGHT on CA Hwy 190.
4 Drive 30 miles to Furnace Creek Visitor Center

Ghost Town Route

160 miles

3 hours

1 From Interstate 15, EXIT on Hwy 95 North.
2 Drive 120 miles to Beatty, Nevada. TURN LEFT on NV Hwy 374
3 Drive 19 miles to Hells Gate. TURN LEFT on Beatty Cutoff Road.
4 Drive 10 miles. TURN LEFT on CA Hwy 190
5 Drive 11 miles to Furnace Creek Visitor Center.

Most Scenic Route

172 miles

3.5 hours

1 From Interstate 15 South , EXIT on NV Hwy 160 West
2 Drive 45 miles. TURN LEFT on Tecopa Road
3 Drive 41 miles. TURN RIGHT on CA Hwy 127
4 Drive 10 miles. TURN LEFT on CA Hwy 178 West
5 Drive 75 miles. TURN LEFT on CA Hwy 190.
6 Drive one mile to Furnace Creek Visitor Center.

ACCOMMODATIONS

The 2 types of accommodation within the park include lodging with food or camping. Some of the lodges also have other facilities such as a bar, fuel, and general store. They are all open year-round. The 4 options are:

- *Stovepipe Wells Village*: 760-786-7090
- *Oasis at Death Valley* (Inn or Ranch): 800-236-7916

- *Panamint Springs Resort*: 775-482-7680

Campground options depend on the time of year:

April 16–October 14: Due to excessive heat, only campgrounds at higher elevations where it is slightly cooler are open:

- Mesquite Spring
- Emigrant
- Wildrose

October 15–April 15: All campgrounds are first-come-first-serve except for Furnace Creek where reservations can be made during peak season up to 6 months in advance: *Furnace Creek campground reservations.*

Other campgrounds vary in size and services. Some have hookups, all have toilets, and most have water. The fees, which are payable at automatic machines with credit or debit cards, vary from free to $60 for an RV hookup. Camping facilities include:

- Sunset (largest — often has spots left during peak season)
- Texas Springs
- Fiddler's
- Stovepipe Wells RV Park
- Stovepipe Wells Park Service
- Thorndike
- Mahogany Flat
- Panamint Springs

Pets are welcome in the built-up areas, roads, campgrounds, and picnic areas (not on the trails), but they must be always kept on a leash.

PARK ATTRACTIONS

- There are a range of sightseeing *Death Valley activities* as outlined below.
- Furnace Creek visitor center: Start here at the central hub for Death Valley with rangers, museum, bookstore, and 20-minute film.

Furnace Creek is actually a small village that offers modern amenities and activities like golf, swimming, and tennis.

- Mesquite Flat sand dunes: East of Stovepipe Wells, these sand dunes set against steep mountains create amazing shadows. They are diverse and ever changing with some as high as 100 feet.
- Dante's View: At 5,478 feet above sea level, this is an ideal location to escape the heat and take in panoramic views of the southern half of Death Valley. The valley goes for as far as the eye can see, and you can marvel at mountains, flat sands, and dunes.
- Badwater Basin: In the south of Death Valley, this is the lowest point in the western hemisphere at 277 feet below sea level. The basin stretches for nearly 200 square miles over fragile salt flats. Depending on the time of year, Badwater Lake may have enough water for some epic photography.
- The Racetrack: In the remotest part of the valley with dry, barren land, the only disturbance here are tracks made by "sailing stones." There is speculation about how the rocks moved, some believing it was wind and rainwater, others by floating ice.
- Zabriskie Point: Millions of years ago, there was a flowing lake here, which, along with the weather, caused the erosion visible today. The rich yellows and browns of the badlands are exaggerated by the Black Mountains in the background.
- Artist's Drive and Artist's Palette: Between Furnace Creek and Badwater, the 9-mile Artist's Drive Road takes you to Artist's Palette. Oxidation of metals in the hillsides has created hues of orange, pink, brown, teal, purple and blue.
- International Dark Sky Park: Download the _SkyView App_.
- _Cycling_: There are around 300 miles of roads suitable for biking or mountain biking.

For any outing, activity, or hike, make sure you have plenty of water and protection from the sun. Let's move on to the hikes.

TOP HIKING TRAILS – LOCATIONS, SPECIFICATIONS,
ACTIVITIES AND SITES

Beginner Trails

Badwater Salt Flats Trail

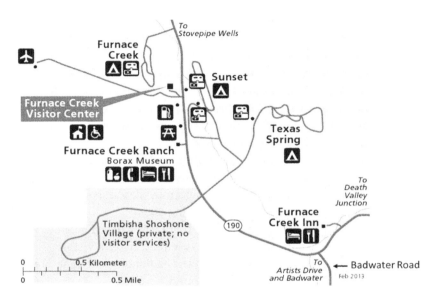

- The trailhead begins off Badwater Road south of 190 and Furnace Creek. There is parking at the Badwater Basin lot.
- 1.9 miles out-and-back, 6.5 feet elevation change, 30 minutes.
- Paved route – wheelchair and stroller accessible.
- Well signed and practically straight all the way to the flat salts.
- Walk around the salt flats that glisten like snow.
- Marvel at the surrounding mountains and observe the cliff that shows the sea level to give you some perspective.
- Hike at sunrise and sunset because of lower temperatures.

Zabriskie Point Trail

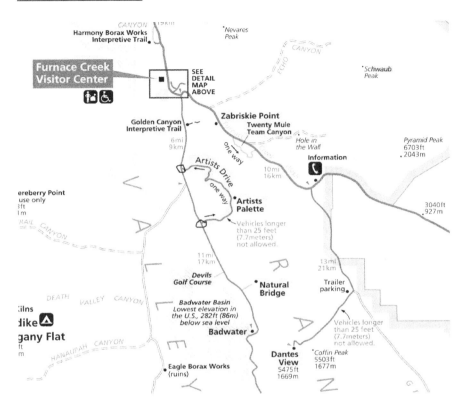

- From Furnace Creek, take 190 east to the trailhead that has parking.
- 0.37 miles out-and-back, 49 feet elevation change, 15 minutes.
- Wheelchair and stroller accessible, however, there is a slightly steeper part where help might be needed.
- Another excellent option for sunrise or sunset where you can stargaze after sunset.
- The trail's end offers some of the best views of Death Valley.

Mesquite Flat Sand Dunes Trail

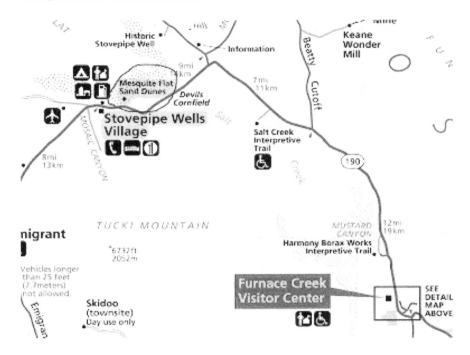

- Head north on 190 from Furnace Creek toward Stovepipe Wells. The trailhead is 2 miles before Stovepipe with a parking lot on the right.
- 2.8 miles out-and-back, 206 feet elevation change, 1–1.5 hours.
- Cover up if it is windy as the sand can sting.
- Well marked trail straight north to the sand dunes – wheelchair and stroller accessible.
- The sand dunes are a place for the whole family to have fun exploring since there is no official trail in the dunes.
- Late afternoon sun provides some excellent opportunities for photography and optical illusions.

Dante's View Trail

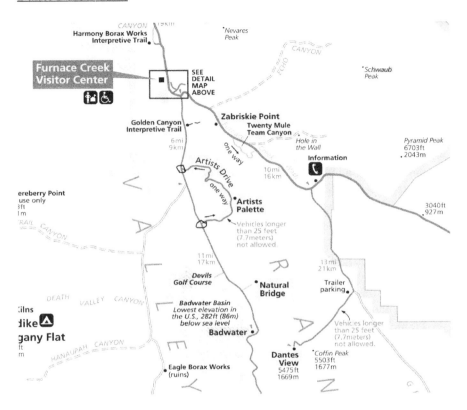

- The trailhead is a 45-minute drive from Furnace Creek off 190. Head southeast for 11 miles, turn right onto Furnace Creek Wash Road (turns into Dante's View Road), and continue for 13 miles to the parking area.
- 1 mile out-and-back, 223 feet elevation change, 30–45 minutes.
- Level sidewalk to overlook – wheelchair and stroller accessible.

  o 2 other less accessible paths are half a mile north climbing rocky slopes with 300 feet elevation change, and east to Coffin's Peak (2 miles out-and-back).

- Spectacular views and photography opportunities atop the ridge of the Black Mountains 5,575 feet above Badwater Basin.

  - "I don't pay much attention to scenery, but I know one view that made me stop and look." 1926: Charles Brown, a local man from Shoshone, when asked by the governor of Nevada for his opinion of the best view of Death Valley.

- On a clear day, you may see the entire 140 miles of Death Valley itself (spans north from the head of Last Chance Canyon to the south at the big bend in Amargosa River near Saratoga Springs). There are also 260° views of Panamint Mountains to the west, Funeral Mountains to the north, Greenwater Range to the east, and Owlshead Mountains to the south.
- Head slightly north along the rim to find solitude. Despite the crowds, this is known as one of the quietest places in California.
- Visit at night with a telescope for star or planet gazing. During a new moon, you will likely see the Milky Way, while a full moon illuminates the salt flats below.
- Picnic tables are at the viewpoint, so pack food to enjoy the scenery a little longer.

Intermediate Trails

Mosaic Canyon

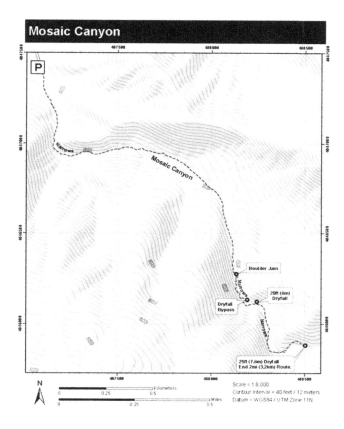

- Ample parking is at the trailhead in front of Stovepipe Wells campground.
- Stop off at the Stovepipe general store for a bathroom and supplies.
- 4 miles out-and-back, 1,200 feet elevation change, 2.5–3 hours.
- Not paved – wheelchair and stroller accessible if you watch out for some larger rocks.
- Starts with smooth, marbled rocks that transition into mosaic breccia, small rocks that have naturally cemented together to form larger rocks.

- For some, the route ends at approximately 1.3 miles with a boulder jam. For others it is possible to squeeze through the boulders to the left.
- A little further on, there is a 20-foot-high dry fall. It's not recommended to climb this. Instead, go back around 180 feet and look to the west where there is a bypass that will take you to the canyon.
- Extend the hike to scramble a bit.

Badlands, Golden Canyon, Red Cathedral, and Gower Gulch

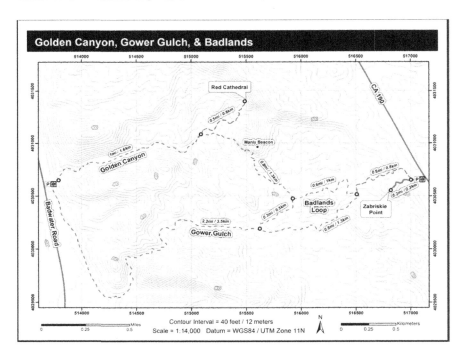

- Badlands loop:

  - The trailhead is at Zabriskie Point parking lot off CA–190, 3.5 miles east of Badwater Road.
  - 2.7-mile loop, 535 feet elevation change, 1.5–2 hours.

- Golden Canyon to Red Cathedral:

  - The trailhead is at Golden Canyon parking lot off Badwater Road, 2 miles south of CA-190.
  - 3 miles out-and-back, 577 feet elevation change, 1.5–2 hours.

- Gower Gulch loop:

  - The trailhead is at the Golden Canyon parking lot.
  - 4.3-mile loop, 850 feet elevation change, 2.5 hours. Adding this trail to Red Cathedral adds 1 mile.

- Entire Trail – Advanced:

  - The trailhead is at Golden Canyon parking lot.
  - Hike Golden Canyon to Red Cathedral to Zabriskie Point to Gower Gulch.
  - 7.8-mile loop, 850 feet elevation change, 4.5 hours.

- At the Golden Canyon trailhead is a clear sign with 4 hiking options so you can choose the best route for your group.
- Scout large chunks of pavement that were part of the road that ran through the canyon.
- See Telescope Peak, the highest point in Death Valley, along with Manly Beacon, named after the man who said "Goodbye, Death Valley"!
- Scramble over 4-foot rocky ledges on the Gower Gulch trail.

Advanced Trails

Telescope Peak Trail

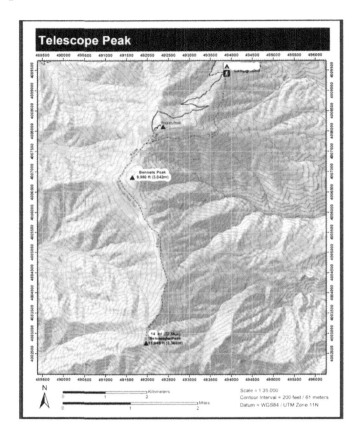

- The trailhead begins at the Mahogany Flat Campground where Emigrant Canyon Road ends. A high clearance 4 x 4 vehicle is needed to get into the campground. Low clearance vehicles best park at Charcoal Kilns and walk to the trailhead.
- 14 miles out-and-back, 3,000 feet elevation change, 7 hours.
- Check with *Telescope Peak* prior to leaving in case of road closures due to weather.
- Expect snow in winter. It is highly recommended to have hiking poles and crampons/ice cleats.
- Mahogany Flat is the last chance to use the bathroom, but bear in mind there is no water available at the camp.

- Starts with a steady climb as you ascend Panamint Mountains.
- Inhale the scents of pinyon pine and mountain mahogany before breaking through to the first impressive view of the valley within 1 mile. After the obstructed view, it might surprise you that you are 8,000 feet up!
- The trail takes you past Rogers Peaks, Bennett Peak, Hanaupah Canyon, and Arcane Meadows. You may camp overnight in this meadow between Rogers and Benner Peaks instead of doing a day hike.
- Before reaching the incredible height of 11,049 feet above sea level at Telescope Peak, you will see limber pines that can live for over 2,000 years and bristlecones pines that are some of the oldest living things on earth at over 5,000 years old!

Dante's Ridge (Mount Perry)

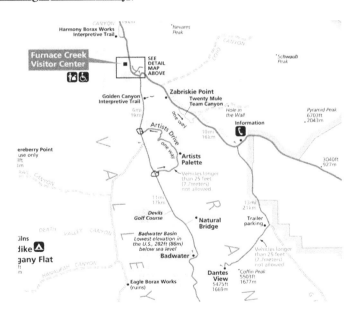

- The trailhead is a 45-minute drive from Furnace Creek off 190. Head southeast for 11 miles, turn right onto Furnace Creek Wash Road (turns into Dante's View Road), and continue for 13 miles to the parking area.
- Extension of Dante's View if you are an advanced hiker.
- 8 miles out-and-back, 2,090 feet of elevation, 4–6 hours.

- There is no shade from the summer sun, so it is advisable to hike prior to 10:00 AM. Winter can bring snow and strong winds.
- You will need to ascend Dante's Peak on the return hike, so energy and water should be saved.
- Most of the trail is easily visible and follows the ridge crest. You can avoid some of the higher points by hiking around them.
- From Dante's View, the trail heads north with the valley to the left. As you follow the ridge, you will have breathtaking views of Panamint Range, Telescope Peak, Badwater Basin, and Pyramid Peak.
- You will know when you reach Mount Perry's base because you can visualize a big bump in the ridgeline. Closing in on this, you will see the old mining town of Ryan in Green Water Valley.
- Ascend Mount Perry. At the summit, the northern valley, and a full view of the amazing ridgeline back to Dante's Peak become visible.
- Scrambling opportunity during the last few 100 feet.

Death Valley National Park is akin to stepping onto another planet with endless views of color and terrain. Nighttime is just as picturesque with formidable star gazing. However, there is scarce shade while hiking, and the temperatures do soar. Take more water than you think necessary and protection from the elements.

Of all the Things to Crave, Aren't You Glad You're Hooked on Hiking, Nature, And the Wonders of National Parks?

"Of all the paths you take in life, make sure a few of them are dirt."

— *JOHN MUIR*

Sadly, few are in the position to give up work and spend their entire days hiking through these mind-blowing scenes. But if you have taken your first adventure in one of these parks, you have an advantage over those who haven't. You have caught the hiking bug!

Monday to Friday is often a long slug fighting your way through the rat race and responsibilities. Your colleagues are discussing their plans for the weekend, and it all sounds like more of the usual routine. You, however, have this burning desire to trade office shoes for boots and head off on your next hike.

It's true that the first hike may have been a learning curve. It's normal to not feel as confident as desired or nervous that something might go wrong, but the moment you step onto a trail, nature has a way of taking over. There is so much to take in and observe that everything that was previously on your mind just drifts away.

An escape to a national park exposes you to a tranquility that is hard to find in day-to-day life. The sounds of nature are crisp, the colors are vibrant, and the air is pure. It doesn't matter if you have made it to the tallest summit or crossed the lowest valley; each corner you turn has a new treat for your senses.

Even when Monday comes around again, the power of nature stays with you heading back to the routine with a new perspective. Now, it's time to pass on that joy to others.

By sharing your opinions and hiking adventures on Amazon, others can take their first steps to America's magnificence with all the knowledge they need.

After all, there is plenty of nature for us all to enjoy and wouldn't it be nice if everyone could experience these benefits and be a little happier! It only takes a couple of minutes, and I will be very grateful.

CHAPTER 7: JOSHUA TREE NATIONAL PARK

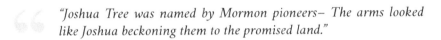

"Joshua Tree was named by Mormon pioneers— The arms looked like Joshua beckoning them to the promised land."

— *DIANA HOLLINGSWORTH GESSLER*

CONTACT INFORMATION

Website: *General Information*

Phone Number: 760-367-5500

Address: (Mailing) 74485 National Park Drive, Twentynine Palms, CA, 92277

PARK OVERVIEW

The park stretches over 1,240 square miles where the Mojave and Sonoran deserts meet. These different terrains sink toward Coachella Valley close to Palm Springs. The western side of the Sonoran Desert is considered the low desert with more enjoyable temperatures for hiking. The Mojave Desert is wetter with more vegetation including the Joshua trees. The terrain was crafted millions of years ago after the last ice age, likely from extreme temperatures combined with wind and heavy rain.

Joshua Tree was established as a national park in 1994 attracting 2.8 million visitors annually. Aside from the 50 different species of mammals, the Joshua trees, and other plants, this national park is perfect for scenic sunsets, sunrises, and stargazing.

PLANNING

You can see the main attractions in Joshua Tree in a few hours, so it's a convenient park if you are short on time. There is ample camping if you do wish to stay longer.

Spring is the best season to visit with daytime temperatures between 70–80ºF. Even at night, it's still a comfortable 40–50ºF. In summer, the heat can be overwhelming, reaching over 100ºF. Winter temperatures are rather mild between 37–58ºF, and you will be able to avoid crowds.

There is public Wi-Fi in the 2 visitor centers, the Joshua Tree visitor center inside Joshua Tree and the Oasis visitor center in Twentynine Palms. You won't be able to access internet throughout the park, so it's best to take physical maps. Cell phone coverage is also weak to non-existent.

ADMISSION AND FEES

Fees & Passes

Like many national parks, there are 5 free days to enter, and you can use your America the Beautiful passes to enter.

Other fees include:

- Vehicles – $30
- Motorcycle – $25
- Individuals – $15
- Annual Pass – $55
- Annual Senior Pass – $20
- Lifetime Senior Pass – $80

You can buy passes online using the link above or in person. There are 2 park entrances where you can pay by card. The previously mentioned visitor centers as well as the Cottonwood visitor center allow you to buy passes with cash or card.

DIRECTIONS

The park is just a few hours from Los Angeles, San Diego, Las Vegas, and Phoenix.

Flying:

The closest airport is in Palm Springs, California: *Palm Springs International Airport*

Public Transport:

Catch a bus from Los Angeles Downtown, Los Angeles Union Station, or East Los Angeles, all passing through Indigo. You can book tickets via *Rome2Rio* or *Basin Transit*.

Driving:

There are 3 park entrances:

- West Entrance: 5 miles south of Highway 62 and Park Boulevard junction at Joshua Tree Village.
- North Entrance: 3 miles south of Highway 62 and Utah Trail junction in Twentynine Palms.
- South Entrance: 25 miles east of Indigo, I-10 near Cottonwood Spring.

ACCOMMODATIONS

There are numerous options for accommodation in the area, from hotels to camping or "glamping".

- *Joshua Tree Inn*
- *Joshua Tree Ranch House*
- *Sacred Sands*
- *The Castle House: Estate*

Reserved _campgrounds_ in the park; call 877-444-6777 or check _HipCamp_.

- Black Rock – $25 per night, flush toilets, water
- Cottonwood – $25 per night, flush toilets, water
- Indian Cove – $25 per night, pit toilets, no water
- Jumbo Rocks – $20 per night, pit toilets, no water
- Ryan – $20 per night, pit toilets, no water
- Sheep Pass Group – $35–$50 per night, vault toilets, no water

First come first serve Campsites:

- Hidden Valley – pit toilets, no water
- White Tank – vault toilets, no water
- Belle – pit toilets, no water

These sites cost $15 per night. Secure a campsite and head to the entrance stations to pay and register.

Camping Outside the Park:

- _Joshua Tree Lake_ RV & Campground
- _Twentynine Palms RV Resort_
- _Palm Springs/Joshua Tree KOA_

Pets are allowed in the camping and picnic areas. Generally, they are allowed on roads where you can drive your car, however, it's prohibited to leave dogs in the car.

PARK ATTRACTIONS

- Joshua Tree _shops and farmers market_: Local shop hours vary but the farmers market is open each Saturday morning.
- Joshua Tree music festival: Annual _music festival_ held during 4 days and nights in May and October. The annual _Coachella Valley_ music and arts festival spans 2 weekends in April and is about 30 minutes driving distance from the park in Indio, California.
- Hidden Valley: This is one of the most accessible areas of the park with a lovely picnic area, Joshua trees to marvel at, and boulders and rock piles that are popular for climbing.

- Keys View: Visit this lookout with an elevation of over 5,000 feet offering stunning views of Coachella Valley, San Andreas fault line, Palm Springs, Salton Sea, and on super clear days, even Mexico.
- Cholla cactus garden: This garden houses thousands of densely packed chollas, tree-like cacti that can grow up to 8 feet tall.
- Skull Rock: Here, you will find rolling rock piles for walking or light scrambling, most notably the naturally formed rock shaped like a giant skull.
- Cottonwood visitor center: This remote *visitor center* often serves as the starting point for exploring Cottonwood Spring, a result of earthquake activity. This area is one of the best in the park for birdwatching.
- *Blackrock nature center*: Visit the art gallery and purchase maps, books, and guides.
- *Rock climbing:* Over 8,000 climbing routes offer climbing, bouldering, highlining, and slacklining experiences for all skill levels on monzogranite rock formations.
- *Horseback riding:* Rentals are available from 3 locations or bring your own horse with you to Ryan or Black Rock Equestrian campgrounds.
- *Cycling:* Biking or mountain biking is allowed on roads open to vehicles and Ryan campground has 3 sites for cyclists.

TOP HIKING TRAILS

Beginner Trails

Arch Rock Trail

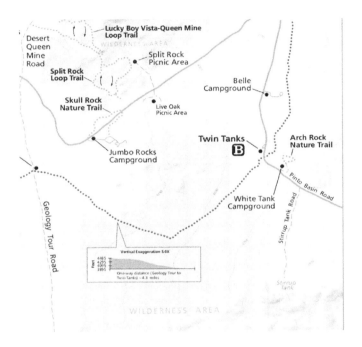

- The trailhead is at the parking lot off Pinto Basin Road by White Tank campground.
- 1.3-mile lollipop loop, 88 feet elevation change, 30 minutes.
- Natural, relatively flat path around 4 feet wide – wheelchair and stroller accessible.
- Heading south for a few 100 feet, you will come to a junction at the beginning of the loop where you can choose to proceed either way.
- Various informational placards educate about geological history.
- Arch rock is a 30-foot-tall arch that has been shaped by the elements. There are other rocks for scrambling and scaling for photo ops.
- Start earlier in the morning or later in the evening if hiking this popular trail during peak spring season.

Barker Dam Trail

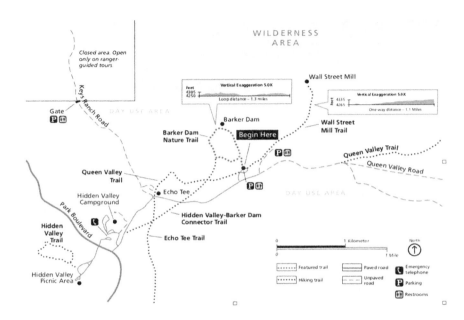

- Located about 13 miles southeast of the west entrance. Park at the trailhead off Keys Ranch Road or closer to Queen Valley trail and follow the signs.
- 1.1-mile lollipop loop, 50 feet elevation change, 30–45 minutes.
- Suitable for children but not wheelchairs or strollers due to granite boulders and steps to traverse as the path progresses. (Strollers are actually not allowed to preserve the trail).
- Informational placards educate regarding desert plants, animals, and people.
- If there has been rain, the dam might have water.
- You may spot bighorn sheep, reptiles, or birds.
- Observe petroglyphs on the rock formations.

Hidden Valley Trail

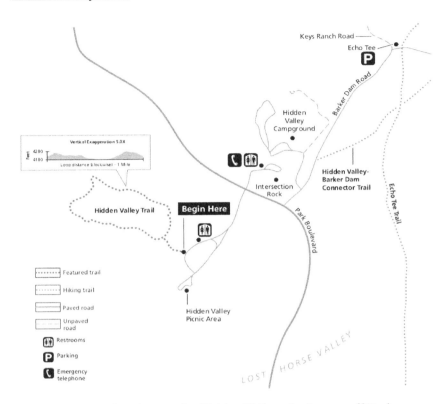

- The trailhead is close to the Hidden Valley picnic area off Park Boulevard. Although the parking lot is large, it fills up quickly.
- 1-mile loop, 118 feet elevation change, 30–45 minutes.
- Suitable for children.
- The trail's beginning elevates quickly as you pass through a narrow canyon.
- This valley of rocks is well sheltered away from the hustle and bustle of the main road.
- Intersection Rock is close to the trailhead if you enjoy rock climbing.
- Rock towers and cliffs are made of monzogranite rock that was formed over 100 million years ago. Magma cooled, and then over the years water erosion caused interesting formations.
- Golden rock formations surround the valley.
- Stunning views with plenty of Joshua trees to admire.

Split Rock Loop

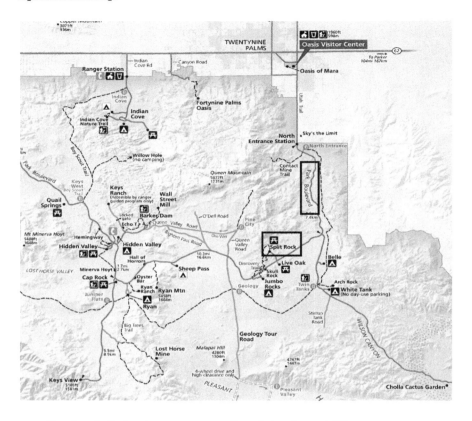

- Head to Split Rock picnic area off Park Boulevard. There is no paved parking lot, so park your car on the side of the road.
- 2.4-mile loop, 275 feet elevation change, 45–60 minutes.
- Well maintained – suitable for children.
- Extend the hike via the fork on the eastern side of the loop out to Face Rock.
- Ideal for trail runners, bird watchers, and nature enthusiasts.
- Walk through some of the densest rock formations in the park, many of which resemble images of something. Look out for sleeping turtle rock!
- Monzogranite rock formations yield a natural playground with abundant photo ops.

Intermediate Trails

Fortynine Palms Oasis Trail

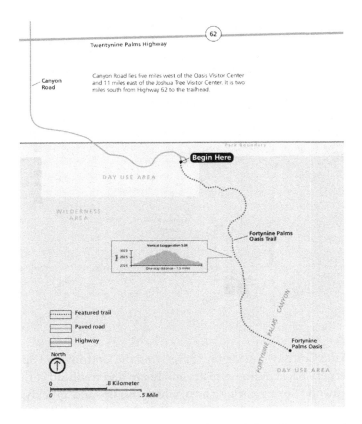

- From Canyon Road, follow the signs for 49 Palms Canyon and stay left at the fork to arrive at parking.
- 3.1 miles out-and-back, 636 feet elevation change, 1.5–2 hours.
- Suitable for older children.
- The path inclines up a small mountain first and then continues along ridgelines until it descends to the oasis.
- Don't forget that you will have to ascend back out!
- Spot wildlife such as rabbits and coyotes at this iconic 49 Palms water source. The oasis, trail, and parking are seasonally closed during summer to provide bighorn sheep with undisturbed water access.
- Find barrel cacti growing on ridges.

- This is a shaded area of the park that is a nice rest stop and picnic; just don't leave anything behind.

Lost Palms Oasis

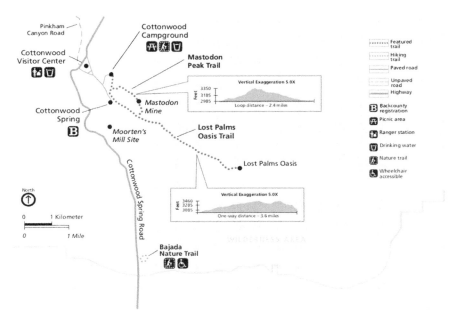

- From the Cottonwood visitor center, find the Cottonwood Spring Wilderness Backcountry registration board and trailhead at the Cottonwood Spring parking area, which fills up quite quickly. Hit the bathrooms at the visitor center since there are no toilets at the trailhead.
- 7.5 miles out-and-back, 500 feet elevation change, 3 hours.
- Well signed trail with a mixture of rock, dirt, and sand.
- Light scrambling opportunity.
- Descend steps to Cottonwood Spring Oasis and head southeast over rolling desert hills for 3.5 miles.
- Continue until the path drops to a flat plateau and then an overlook of the palms.
- The oasis is sprinkled with California fan palms, which are actually the only native palm trees in California, along with barrel cacti, ocotillo, and wildflowers.

- From the plateau above Lost Palms Oasis, you can view mountains in the distance as well as fan palms growing on the cliff sides and Dike Springs to the north.
- Extend the hike at the junction of Mastodon Peak, which offers a scrambling opportunity to the top of the peak where you get to see the Mastodon Mine ruins and Winona village.
- You can also extend the trail onto Victory Palms, which requires scrambling experience.

Ryan Mountain Trail

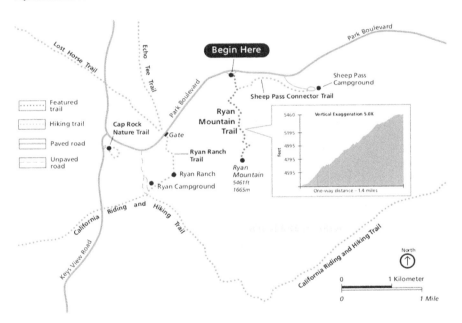

- The trailhead is between Ryan and Sheep Pass campgrounds off Park Boulevard.
- There is a second trailhead at Sheep Pass, but there is no parking unless you are camping there.
- 3 miles out-and-back trail, 1,050 feet elevation change, 1.5–2 hours.
- Easy to follow, but rugged and uneven with several steps to climb.
- At the trailhead, you can explore a large rock formation and discover details about early native settlers.
- Start ascending the rock staircase and look back at the Wonderland of Rocks.

- After a steep beginning, the trail levels out along the ridge where much of the trail is only wide enough for one person.
- Making your way to the top of Ryan Mountain will involve some more jagged rocks, but this is well worth it for the spectacular panoramic views.
- Some parts of the trail are suitable for trail running.

Advanced Trails

Warren Peak via Black Rock Trail and Panorama Loop

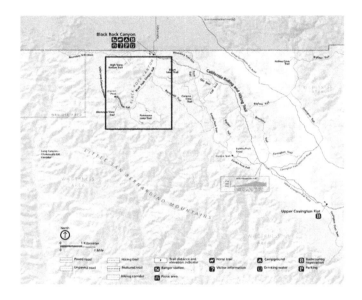

- This lesser explored hike starts at the parking lot near Black Rock campground.
- Black Rock trail + Panorama loop: 6.8 miles, 1, 195 feet elevation change, 3– 3.5 hours
- Black Rock trail + Panorama loop + Warren Peak: 8 miles 1,750 feet elevation change, 3.5–4 hours.
- Well signed and easy to follow to the Burnt Hill junction before joining the Black Rock trail.
- For the best views, head clockwise around the loop.
- Mostly sandy with switchbacks, and then the path starts to get steeper. Don't miss the turnoff for Warren Peak at mile 4.4, which is a hard right by a big tree in the middle of the trail.

- A marvelous range of terrains passes through Black Rock Canyon, home to desert bees and various other wildlife.
- The high elevation fosters more vegetation than other parts of the park making it green with Joshua trees, juniper, piñon pine, oak trees, foxtail, and beavertail cacti. In bloom, the colors are eye-catching.
- Part of the trail follows the ridge of the Little San Bernardino Mountains.
- As you climb, you will view San Gorgonio, Mojave National Preserve, and Mount San Jacinto.
- Popular for horseback riding and trail running.

Geology Tour Road

- The turnoff for Geology Tour Road is near Jumbo Rocks campground where you can park.
- 18-mile lollipop loop, 700 feet elevation change, 7 hours.
- It is only recommended between October and April.
- Paved road for around 100 feet before it turns to dirt. Here, there is a map that you can photograph.
- The scenic drive option is about 2 hours by car if you have a 4 x 4. Take an emergency vehicle repair kit just in case.
- The loop part of the road goes through Pleasant Valley and must be driven in a clockwise direction.
- Squaw Tank is at mile 6 with many boulders, and after a short walk you can see a concrete wall from an old dam among the rocks.
- There is a backcountry camping area if you wish to stay. Otherwise, continue to Cottonwood Springs. 2 old water tanks signal that the road is about to get narrow and bumpy.
- Fun for mountain biking and walking your leashed dog.

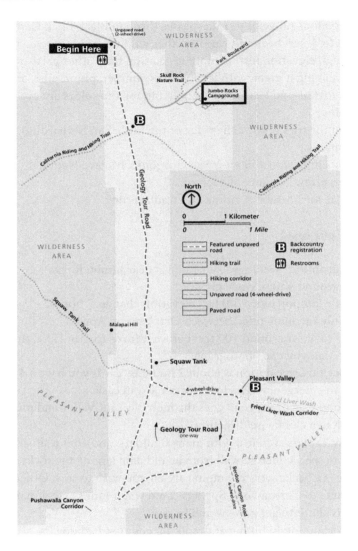

Boy Scout Trail

- Park at the Keys West trailhead and continue onto Boy Scout trail and Indian Cove Road.
- 8 miles point-to-point from Keys West to Indian Cove or vice versa, or 16 miles out-and-back, 531 feet elevation change, 3–4 hours each way.
- There is parking at both trailheads to facilitate a point-to-point hike with 2 vehicles (or a drop off and pickup of hikers).
- There is a pit toilet at the Keys West trailhead, but no water. Water can be obtained at the opposite end of the trail at the Indian Cove ranger station.
- There are numerous hikes branching off the trail, all of which are well marked.

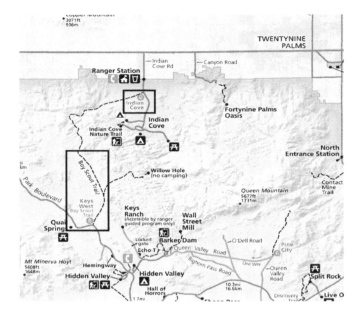

- Some parts have loose boulders, so trekking poles might be useful.
- Especially early in the morning, you may spot bighorn sheep, coyotes, or jackrabbits.
- Hike through Wonderland of Rocks, a perfect exploration spot, but be careful not to get lost on the trail.
- Look out for an old water basin, a relic from the mining days in the area.
- Many photo opportunities with views of San Gorgonio Mountain, part of 29 Palms, canyons, washes, and, of course, Joshua trees!

Joshua Tree National Park has a little bit of something for everyone, and it's an easy park to explore in a day. Combine shorter hikes to take in wildlife and unique vegetation. Bring out your inner child while climbing over the boulders. While many of the beginner trails get quite crowded, you can still find more secluded areas.

* * *

Next up, we are going to look at 2 national parks that share miles of border and are therefore managed as one park.

CHAPTER 8: KINGS CANYON AND SEQUOIA NATIONAL PARKS

"The sequoias belong to the silences of the millennials. Many of them have seen a hundred human generations rise, give off their little claymore and perish. They seem indeed to be forms of immortality standing here among the transitory shapes of time."

— EDWIN MARKHAM

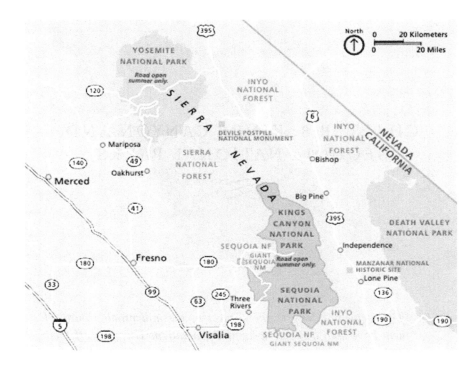

CONTACT INFORMATION

Website: *General Information*

Phone Number: 559-565-3341

Address: 47050 Generals Highway, Three Rivers, CA 93271

PARK OVERVIEW

Kings Canyon and Sequoia National Park (managed as one park) are just east of central California, and both house some of the largest organisms in the world. Highlights include rapid rivers, mountains, impressive groves of giant sequoias, meadows, and different wildlife.

In 1890, President Benjamin Harrison established Sequoia as the country's second national park consisting of 631 square miles set in the Sierra Nevada with elevations of up to 8,500 feet. This park protects the giant sequoias, some of the largest and oldest organisms in the world. General

Sherman is the largest tree and is estimated at 2,300–2,700 years old! There are numerous other tree species as well as wildflowers and animals, such as black bears, mule deer, and gray foxes.

A week after establishing Sequoia, the president added General Grant National Park; however, in 1940, President Franklin D. Roosevelt established Kings Canyon National Park absorbing General Grant Park. Covering 721 square miles, inside is General Grant, the world's second largest tree, which is among 1,200 species of other vegetation. Most of Kings Canyon is over a mile deep with heights reaching 8,200 feet making it deeper than the Grand Canyon!

PLANNING

Although many hikes can be completed in 1 day, it's best to plan for at least 2 days to enjoy a full day at each park. Reserve _wilderness permits_ up to 6 months in advance during quota season between mid-May and mid-September. Walk up wilderness permits may also be available starting at 1:00 PM the day before your trip through rangers at trailhead desks.

The weather is appealing to those who struggle with desert temperatures. July and August are the warmest months with average highs of around 70ºF making these months the busiest. The lowest winter temperatures are around 20ºF with a chance for snow. Avoid hiking crowds from November to April, but camping is more favorable during spring and summer.

There are 2 visitor centers in the park, Kings Canyon visitor center in Grant Grove and Foothills visitor center near the entrance to Sequoia National Park. There is free Wi-Fi here and in the park lodges. Throughout the park, cell coverage is often limited.

ADMISSION AND FEES

Fees & Passes

7-day passes are valid for both parks. Passes can be bought online in advance or at the entrances with cash, but they do prefer cards.

Fees for the passes are:

- Vehicle – $35
- Individual – $20
- Motorcycle – $30
- Annual pass – $70

It's worth noting that 80% of the entrance and camping fees go back into improving the park. You can also visit for free on one of the 5 days that all national parks offer no entrance fees or use your America the Beautiful pass. Those with a 4th grader can access the parks for free through the Every Kid Outdoors Program.

DIRECTIONS

Flying:

There are 2 airports that are a few hours' drive from the parks.

- Fresno, California: *Fresno Yosemite International Airport*
- Visalia, California: *Visalia Municipal Airport*

Public Transport:

Several bus and train routes conveniently connect to the *Sequoia shuttle service* in Visalia, which runs only during the summer.

- *Greyhound* offers a bus from Fresno Greyhound Station to Visalia Transit Center.
- The City of Visalia's *V-Line* is another bus route from Fresno Yosemite Airport to the Visalia Transit Center.
- An additional bus route by *Tulare County area transit* runs from Visalia Transit Center to the Memorial Building in Three Rivers.

- There are *Amtrak* train stations at Hanford and Fresno where cars can be rented for the 1 hour and 45-minute trip to the park. Hanford also has bus connections to the Visalia Transit Center.

Driving:

- From Fresno, take Highway 180 to the Big Stump entrance to Kings Canyon.
- From Three Rivers, take Highway 198 to the Ash Mountain entrance to Sequoia.
- Access the Lookout Point entrance to Sequoia: Take Mineral King Road from Highway 198 in Three Rivers town 2 miles before Ash Mountain. The narrow, winding road to the remote Mineral King area is not recommended for RVs or trailers and is open seasonally from late May–late October.

ACCOMMODATIONS

There are 4 hotels/lodges in the park. Inside Sequoia is Wuksachi Lodge near General Sherman Tree. There is a restaurant, shop, facilities for special events, and dog friendly rooms. In Kings Canyon, there is John Muir Lodge with stone fireplaces and timber beam ceilings. Grant Grove Cabins offer a more rustic experience, and Cedar Grove Lodge is in the heart of the park. There are only 21 rooms, so early reservations are recommended. Pets are allowed at John Muir Lodge and Grant Cove Cabins but can't be left unattended: *Kings Canyon & Sequoia lodges*, 866-807-3598.

Campgrounds:

- Lodgepole
- Dorset Creek
- Buckeye Flat
- Stony Creek Sequoia
- Upper Stony Creek
- Potwisha
- Cove Group
- Fir Group
- Big Meadow

Prices start from $28 per night and can be booked here through
campgrounds. While bikes and leashed dogs are allowed on the campgrounds, neither are allowed on hiking trails.

PARK ATTRACTIONS

- Grant Grove: This is a sequoia grove with General Grant Tree as its
  centerpiece. Several trailheads are found here, and it is close to
  Grant Grove Village and the visitors center with educational
  exhibits, native American art, park information, a market, and a gift
  shop.
- Grant Grove stables: _Horseback riding_ is a fun way to explore the
  scenic views. Book a 1 or 2-hour guided tour through the giant
  sequoias.
- Cedar Grove: At the bottom of Kings Canyon is one of the most
  stunning and least crowded areas of the park.
- Kings River: Enjoy _swimming, kayaking, and fishing_ with a California
  fishing license. Swimming and kayaking should be done cautiously
  only if you have sufficient skills.
- Boyden Cavern: Take a 50-minute _guided tour_ through this marble
  cave with stalagmites, stalactites, and flowstones passing beneath
  the 2,000-foot-high marble walls of Windy Cliffs and Kings Gate.
- Crescent Meadow: John Muir called this "the gem of the Sierra
  Nevada" where you can take in the Sierra pine woodlands, Tharp's
  Log, and Giant Forest. During summer, colorful blooms burst from
  different wildflowers.
- Crystal Cave: Marvel at unique formations with _guided tours_ from
  50 minutes to 6 hours during May–November organized by
  Sequoia Parks Conservancy. Buy tickets online at least 36 hours in
  advance.
- Roaring River Falls: Just off Highway 180, you can find Roaring
  River Falls and watch the water push through a narrow granite gap
  and then fall 40 feet.

TOP HIKING TRAILS – LOCATIONS, SPECIFICATIONS, ACTIVITIES AND SITES

Beginner Trails

General Grant Tree Trail – Kings Canyon

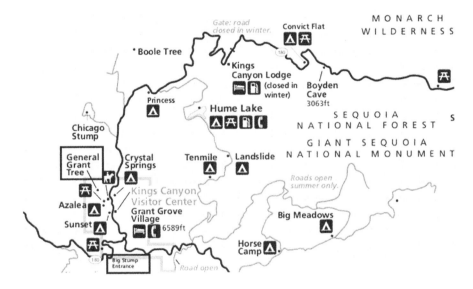

- The parking lot with toilets and water is off Grant Tree Road north of Big Stump entrance.
- 0.8-mile loop, 30 feet elevation change, 20 minutes.
- Paved and 6 feet wide – wheelchair and stroller accessible, although pushing is easier heading clockwise.
- As one of the oldest and most popular areas in the park it's often best to set out after 5 PM to avoid crowds.
- General Grant Tree stands 267 feet tall with a diameter of 29 feet and is the second largest tree in the world.
- Vermont Log is another giant sequoia that has fallen and broken into pieces.
- To the north of General Grant Tree is Gamlin Cabin built in 1872 by Israel Gamlin. He and his brother lived there while their cattle grazed until the U.S. Cavalry used it as a storehouse.
- Other trees of interest include Lightning Tree, Centennial Stump, Oregon Tree, and California Tree.

Zumwalt Meadow and Roaring River Falls – Kings Canyon

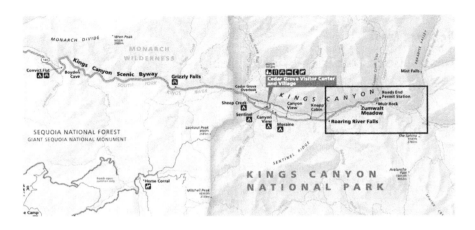

- From the Kings Canyon Scenic Byway, follow signs for the Roaring River Falls trailhead. If the parking area is full, there is overflow parking on the other side of the bridge.
- 5.4 miles out-and-back, 419 feet elevation change, 2–2.5 hours.
- Partially paved – wheelchair and stroller accessible.
- Head south to the falls and then onto Zumwalt Meadow trail, which approaches the Kings River south fork. After crossing a footbridge over a creek, keep right onto the Zumwalt Meadow loop trail. Continue onto the River trail to the route's end and then return the same way.
- The access road to this trail is closed in the winter. In summer and autumn be prepared for bugs.
- Zumwalt Meadow is an idyllic picnic spot where you may spot bears and deer as well as other small mammals, birds of prey, and snakes.
- Admire the vibrant colors of the wildflowers and woodlands including red firs, incense cedars, and pines.
- Roaring River Falls is a magnificent 40-foot waterfall that cascades into a granite gorge.
- Enjoy the peaceful babbling of Kings River.
- Suitable for trail running.

Panoramic Point – Kings Canyon

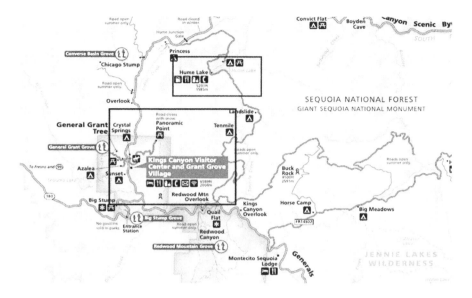

- The trailhead is 2 miles north of Kings Canyon visitor center where Panoramic Point Road dead ends. There is a turn off for parking.
- 0.5-mile lollipop loop, 100 feet elevation change, 30 minutes.
- Paved and 5 feet wide – wheelchair and stroller accessible, but help might be required on a couple of steep inclines.
- Head southeast with a gradual incline. At the intersection, keep left on the paved path to Panoramic Point and then continue south to Park Ridge Viewpoint.
- Either head back the same way to stay on the pavement or join the dirt loop trail heading further south to circle back around.
- Panoramic Point has an elevation of 7,500 feet providing breathtaking views of the Sierra Nevada and Kings Canyon. Informational panels explain the area's history and point out mountain peaks.
- From this viewpoint you can also see Hume Lake, Spanish Mountain, the Obelisk, Mount McGee, Mount Goddard, Kettle Dome, North Palisade, and Eagle Peak.
- There are restrooms, picnic tables, and benches in the area.
- Good for snowshoeing or cross-country skiing in the winter after snow.

General Sherman Tree Trail – Sequoia

- The trailhead is off Wolverton Road with parking between Sherman Tree and Lodgepole.
- With a disability parking placard, you can park in a small lot off Generals Highway where a wheelchair accessible trail leads a short distance to the tree.
- 1.2-miles out-and-back, 196 feet elevation change, 30–45 minutes.
- Paved with a few stairs – suitable for children.
- Since this trail is so popular, early morning is the best time to visit the tree.
- Head through a corridor of conifers and smaller sequoias before reaching an intersection. Stick left to walk further into the woodlands before the General Sherman Tree comes into view.
- General Sherman Tree isn't just impressive for its 275 feet height, it is 35 feet in diameter at its base and estimated to be 6,167 tons! This is the largest tree in the world as measured by volume.
- Take a moment to read about this giant sequoia and absorb the beauty of the area on 1 of the benches dotted along the trail.

- There are abundant wildflowers and possibly black bears if it's quiet.

Intermediate Trails

<u>Mist Falls – Kings Canyon</u>

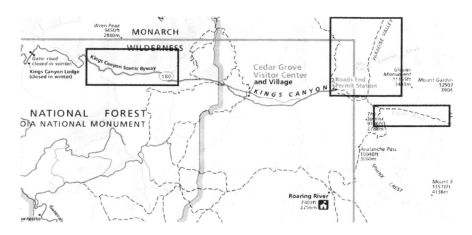

- The trailhead starts at Roads End off Highway 180 (Kings Canyon Scenic Byway). The parking lot fills quickly.
- 8 miles out-and-back, 875 feet elevation change, 3 hours.
- Suitable for older children.
- The trailhead has toilets but no water.
- Bring bug spray to ward off mosquitos!
- Mostly flat until the end of the trail where there is a sharp, rocky 600-foot incline to the falls.
- For a more secluded detour, take the junction to Kings Canyon backcountry 2.6 miles from the trailhead.
- Begins as a lovely hike through woodlands and meadows with marshy areas in spring. Plentiful wildflowers and some nice shade.
- Where the canyon bends at a 90° angle, there is Bubbs Creek along with cascades and rapids.
- Mist Falls provides a refreshing spray after the steep hike.
- Past the falls is a more level section with large flat boulders overlooking Paradise Valley where you can camp.
- While the clear, deep pools look inviting, the current is fast, so swimming isn't recommended.

Big Baldy Ridge – Kings Canyon

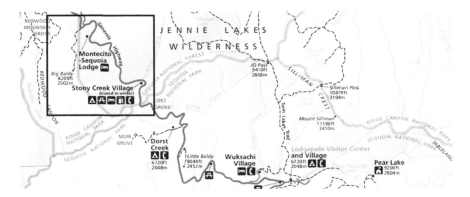

- The trailhead is 5 miles northwest of Stony Creek campground off Generals Highway. There is lay-by parking off the side of the road.
- 4.4 miles out-and-back, 650–foot elevation change, 2.5 hours.
- There are no amenities at the trailhead, so be prepared.
- Heads south through a few steep inclines. At the intersection, keep to the left.
- Shade decreases along the trail.
- You have reached the top when you come to an expanse of rocks and an official United States Geological Survey (U.S.G.S.) marker.
- The first viewpoint of many along the hike is Redwood Canyon with its blanket of fir trees 2,000 feet below.
- From the summit, you can see Redwood Mountain Grove to the north and the peaks of the Great Divide to the east.
- To the southeast is Little Baldy where you can extend your hike to this lower summit, but the trail becomes more difficult.

Big Stump Loop – Kings Canyon

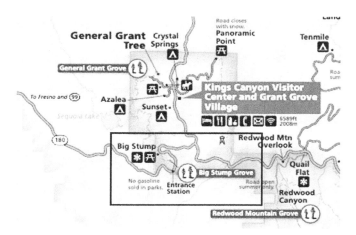

- Park at Big Stump trailhead in the General Grant Grove section near Big Stump entrance.
- 1.5-mile loop, 250 feet elevation change, 1–1.5 hours.
- This is a beginner/intermediate hike because it's a bit hilly and rooty but still suitable for children.
- There are toilets and a picnic area at the trailhead.
- Heads southeastward, and at the junction keep to the left. You will loop around Big Stump to cross the Scenic Bypass.
- Just before the trail joins back onto the loop, cross the bypass again.
- There are informational plaques along the hike.
- While there is more than one big stump, the most significant is the Mark Twain Tree, which grew to 16 feet in diameter before the U.S. Army cut it down in 1891. The tree is now on display in various places such as the American Museum of Natural History and the Natural History Museum, London.
- Climb on Big Stump and other stumps for great photo opportunities and perspective.
- The forest has plentiful wildlife.
- Suitable for trail running.

Moro Rock – Sequoia

- Follow Crescent Meadow Road to Giant Forest Museum where the trail begins. There are 240 parking spaces here, however, on summer weekends the road is closed to private vehicles, so take the *intra-park shuttle bus*.
- 1 mile up 350 concrete steps to the top of Moro Rock, 183 feet elevation change, 20–30 minutes.
- There are handrails on the stairway, but children can easily fall through over steep drop offs. The stairway is closed in winter.
- Besides the stairs, this hike is a bit more challenging due to the altitude adjustment. At 6,725 feet above sea level, you might need to stop and catch your breath.
- Since the rock is prone to lightning strikes, avoid this hike in storms.
- Moro Rock formed millions of years ago when magma beneath the surface of the earth cooled into granite. Since then, erosion has removed the softer layers of rock.
- Boasting some of the best 360° views in the park, you can see the Great Western Divide's peaks, San Joaquin Valley, the southern Sierra, and Giant Forest. On a clear day, you may even be able to see California's Coast Range.
- In summer, Peregrine falcons nest on Moro Rock prompting rock climbing closures from April 1–August 15, however, the stairway remains open.

Marble Falls Trail – Sequoia

- The trailhead is at the Potwisha campground off Generals Highway. Cross the flume to see the trail up the hillside. The campground has parking for cars and RVs, but some roads in the area can't accommodate vehicles over 22 feet long.
- 7.8 miles out-and-back, 1499 feet elevation change, 3.5 hours.
- There is a canal before the sign for the Marble Falls trail at a junction. From this point it is a single track with some switchbacks.
- 2 miles into the hike you will reach a hard bend and Switchback Peak. The trail then starts to descend slightly toward the falls.
- Watch out for poison oak along the trail.
- Diverse terrain from oaklands to mountain views, seasonal creeks, cascades, and waterfalls.
- Swimming in Marble Falls is not recommended because the rocks are slippery and the river can be deadly when the water is high. When the water is low, there are some fun creeks to cross.
- Some parts are suitable for trail running, but exercise caution on uneven ground.

Advanced Trails

Rae Lakes Loop – Kings Canyon

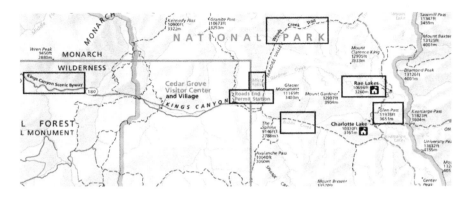

- Obtain a permit at the Roads End trailhead where there is parking.
- 37.6-mile loop, 7,500 feet elevation change, 20 hours.

  - Split this into 3–4 days or longer to spend more time at the waypoints.
  - Alternatively, you can cut the hike in half with the 18-mile Paradise Valley out-and-back trail, camping at either Lower, Middle, or Upper Paradise campgrounds.

- The trailhead has a water bottle filling station, and there is ample fresh water along the hike, but remember to take a water purification system.
- Take the loop either way, but clockwise is easier.
- Head north on the Paradise Valley trail passing Mist Falls, and then continue along the South Fork of King's River. This takes you to Woods Creek trail past Castle Domes Meadow. At the junction, follow the Pacific Crest trail to the series of lakes — Arrowhead and Dollar Lake and the 3 Rae Lakes.
- Past the lakes, you will face Glen Pass. The switchbacks are challenging, but from Vidette Meadow and Bubbs Creek trail back to the trailhead, it's all downhill.
- Camp at Lower, Middle, and Upper Paradise, Rae Lakes, Charlotte Lake, Bullfrog Lake, Arrowhead Lake, and Vidette Meadow. There

are restrictions, so it's best to check at *Rae Lakes camping*. Bring a bear–resistant canister for your food.

- Lower, Middle, and Upper Rae lakes are picture perfect. Green firs contrast the mountains, and sometimes snow tops reflect beautifully in the clear water. Even on a misty morning, the lakes are majestic.
- Woods Creek Bridge is a little rickety but focus on the views above to avoid looking down.
- Charlotte Dome, Bubbs Creek Canyon, and, of course, Kings Canyon are all stunning, as is the Sphinx rock formation at Sphinx Creek.
- Look out for wildlife along with sugar pines, black oaks, Jeffrey pines, and red fir trees.

Mount Gould Trail

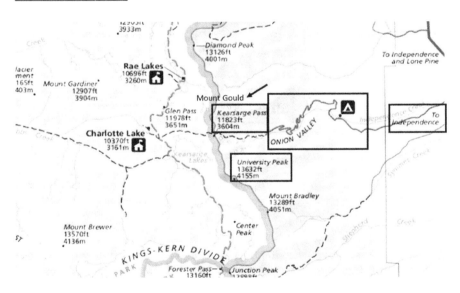

- Onion Valley Road is east of the parks and accessible via Route 395 in Independence, California. Drive west until it ends at Onion Valley campground and Kearsarge Pass trailhead parking area.
- 9 miles out-and-back, 3,773 feet elevation change, 6–7 hours.
- Follow the Kearsarge Pass trail past Gilbert Lake, which is a lovely stop for a rest with Flower and Heart lakes just a little further.

- As you make your way along the switchbacks of Kearsarge Pass, you will see Big Pothole Lake with University Peak in the background to the south.
- Head north from Kearsarge Pass across a boulder field before reaching the south ridge of Mount Gould. There will be some boulder hopping and scrambling all the way to the false summit where you will see a very faint path to the real Mount Gould Summit.
- Popular for birdwatching, wildflower identification, and fishing.

Lakes Trail – Sequoia

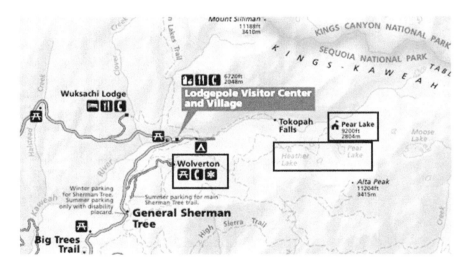

- Start at the Wolverton picnic area and park off Wolverton Road.
- 12.2 miles out-and-back, 2,600 feet elevation change, 7–7.5 hours.
- After about 2 miles of switchbacks through the forest, you will come to a fork in the path where you can follow Hump trail for faster elevation or Watchtower trail if you aren't afraid of heights. The watchtower is a huge spine of rock, and the ridge is narrow with sheer drops. It's not for the faint–hearted but does provide some amazing views.
- Both routes take you to four lakes — Heather, Aster, Emerald, and Pear where you can camp at Emerald and Pear Lakes but check for restrictions.

- Besides camping, make reservations at _Pear Lake winter hut_ open from December to April, accessible only by an advanced level ski trail or snowshoes.
- Watch for black bears and other mammals.
- There are beautiful waterfalls and wildflowers.
- Popular for fishing and horseback riding.

* * *

These two parks offer enough of everything to please the whole family. Aside from the views, the black bears steal the show, and your food, which is why canisters that can be purchased at the visitor centers are required throughout the park.

CHAPTER 9: LASSEN VOLCANIC NATIONAL PARK

"I don't think it is an understatement to say that if it weren't for Frank Loomis, there might not be a Lassen Volcanic National Park. His documentation of the historic eruptions through his glass plate view camera has given USGS scientists invaluable evidence that has helped inform our understanding of the historic eruptions."

— DAVE SCHLOM

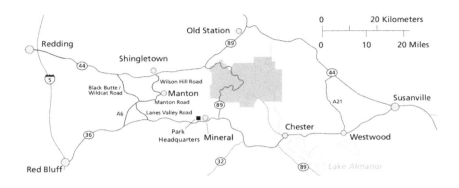

CONTACT INFORMATION

Website: *General Information*

Contact Number: 530-595-4480

Address: 29489 Lassen National Park Hwy, Shingletown, CA 26088

PARK OVERVIEW

Lassen Volcanic National Park is in northern California's wilderness near the small town of Chester and is the perfect destination to enjoy some peace. As its name suggests, there are numerous volcanoes, fumaroles, and boiling mud pots nestled inside forests with crystal clear lakes and expanding meadows.

Established as a national park in 1916, it has the largest plug dome volcano in the world. You will also find the other three types of volcanoes – shield, composite, and cinder cones. This is the only national park that boasts this, meaning it comes with a rich volcanic history and interesting land formations.

As one of California's lesser-known parks with around 400,000 annual visitors, it is an ideal location to escape from large crowds. It is also famous for its world class ranger programs providing plentiful advice and suggestions.

PLANNING

Ideally, plan to spend 2–3 days here because there is so much to explore. The park's high altitude also might make even easier trails more challenging, so you may need more navigation time.

The most popular time to visit is August–September due to ideal temperatures between the upper 70s to mid-80s°F. The park will be busier but not to the extent of previous parks. During winter, the temperatures range from the low 20s to high 50s°F with as much as 30 feet of snow throughout the season, which may close the park highway. On the other hand, the snow offers the chance to enjoy winter sports.

While free Wi-Fi is available at the visitor's center, internet access and cell phone coverage are weak throughout the park. The best coverage is found at Bumpass Hell parking, Lassen Peak parking, and Chaos Jumbles pullout.

ADMISSION AND FEES

Fees & Passes

Use your America the Beautiful Pass for entrance, and families with 4th graders can enter for free. There are also the 5 National Park free days to take advantage of. The fees for a 7-day pass are:

- Vehicle – $30
- Vehicle in winter – $10
- Motorcycle – $25
- Individual – $15
- Annual Pass – $55

Buy passes online at or pay passes at the southwest entrance (new Kohm Yah-mah-nee visitor center) or the northwest entrance (near Loomis Plaza). When these stations are unstaffed, there are self-pay stations outside the entrances.

DIRECTIONS

Before you set off, especially in winter, check the National Park website for *road closures*.

Flying:

- Redding, California: *Redding Regional Airport*
- Sacramento, California: *Sacramento Airport*
- Reno-Tahoe, Nevada: *Reno Airport*

Driving:

There is no public transport to the park so either rent a car or take your own.

- From Redding, take I-5, California 44 Highway straight to the northwest entrance 45 miles from Redding.
- From the south, take California 36 heading east from Red Bluff to arrive at the southwest entrance 51 miles from Red Bluff.
- From Reno, follow the signs for Susanville and join California 44 or California 36, depending on which entrance you want to reach 130 miles from Reno.

The southwest and northwest entrances are connected by Lassen National Park Highway, which is 30 miles long and takes about 1 hour to traverse. There is a strict 35 mph speed limit, which is enforceable via fines.

ACCOMMODATIONS

Drakesbad Guest Ranch is a rustic retreat in the secluded area of Warner Valley. As well as the lodge, bungalows are available, along with a restaurant. Reservations are often booked up to a year in advance online or by calling 877-622-0221.

Rustic cabins are available from late May to mid-October via reservations at *Manzanita Lake campground* or by calling 530-779-0307.

There are 8 campgrounds throughout the park. The first 5 are close to the highway (from north to south) while the other 3 sites are further into the park.

- Manzanita Lake
- Lost Creek
- Summit Lake North
- Summit Lake South
- Southwest
- Warner Valley
- Juniper Lake
- Butte Lake

To camp outside of these grounds, obtain a _backcountry camping permit_. Pets are welcome on the campgrounds and leashed dogs are permitted throughout the park, not on trails. If you leave your dog in the car at trailheads, be sure the temperature isn't too hot, or you may be cited for pet endangerment.

Group campsites require reservations, and for other sites it's recommended to make reservations during peak season between July and September at _campgrounds_. The 2021 Dixie fire caused a lot of damage and affected some of the camping areas; therefore, it's best to consult the National Park Service at the previous link to check for closed campsites.

PARK ATTRACTIONS

- Manzanita Lake: This is the most accessible lake in the park and a perfect spot to wade or even swim but check with park rangers about the potential danger from otters before heading out. From the north shore, there is a perfect photo op with Lassen Peak in the background.
- Boating and fishing: Rent a boat from the _Manzanita Lake camper store_ between 10 AM and 4 PM, or use your own non–motorized vessel on Manzanita, Butte, Juniper, or Summit Lakes. Obtain a permit to fish in these lakes as well.
- Horseback Riding: Guided rides are available from _Drakesbad Guest Ranch_.
- Bumpass Hell: An amazing hydrothermal area named after Kendall V. Bumpass, the first European descendant to visit the area. When he walked off the trail, his foot fell through a crust of ground, burning his foot which is a valuable lesson to us all!

- Sulphur Works: From the southwest entrance, this is the first geothermal area in the park, which was once the location of the 11,000-foot stratovolcano Mount Tehama. Dramatic changes to the area including the formation of the large mud pot left the andesite rock display with colorful sulfur minerals.
- Kings Creek Fall: Along with breathtaking waterfall views close to Lassen Peak, in season, there are wildflowers and wildlife.
- Fantastic Lava Beds: A national monument, volcanic eruptions over the last half million years have resulted in a rugged landscape in this high desert wilderness. There are over 800 caves as well as historic rock art sites and battlefields.
- Stargazing: Removed from the light pollution, this park has clear views of starry nights. In August, there is a 3-day _Dark Sky festival_ and amazing astronomy programs. Download the _SkyView app_.
- Winter sports: Play in the snow, go sledding, or travel over snow via snowshoes, cross-country skiing, backcountry skiing, or snowboarding.

TOP HIKING TRAILS – LOCATIONS, SPECIFICATIONS, ACTIVITIES AND SITES

Beginner Trails

Bumpass Hell Trail

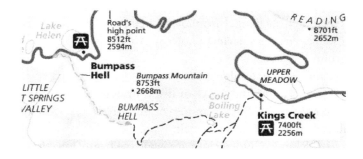

- From the southwest entrance, Bumpass Hell trailhead is well signed from the Lassen Park Highway with a parking lot and toilets.
- 3 miles out-and-back, 433 feet elevation change, 1–1.5 hours.
- As one of the most popular hikes, it's best to head out earlier in the morning to avoid crowds.

- There are informational plaques along the hike.
- Starts north from the parking lot and is relatively flat before heading east past Lassen Peak. Next, head south for a few 100 feet before a sharp turn toward the east.
- As Bumpass Mountain comes into view, cross a creek to arrive at Bumpass Hell's geological feature.
- The trail winds around a 1000-foot-deep valley offering impressive views of Lassen Peak, Lake Helen, Brokeoff Mountain, and Diller Mountain.
- As a hydrothermal geological site, groundwater is heated and turns to steam that escapes geothermal vents creating bubbling pools of water and mud pots.
- The site has guard rails and planks so you can safely explore the dramatic landscapes.
- The sulfur makes for some interesting colors but be prepared for the strong smell.

Manzanita Lake Loop

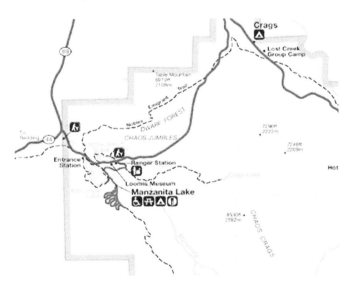

- Trailhead is easy to find from the northwest entrance by Manzanita Creek Campground off the park's highway. There is parking ½ mile past the campground.
- 1.9-mile loop, 52 feet elevation change, 20–30 minutes.

- Mostly paved – wheelchair and stroller accessible.
- Bring sunglasses on bright days as the glare from the lake can be quite intense.
- Just past the Loomis ranger station is a junction. Take the northern path to the northern lakeshore before going south toward the western shore.
- After following the southeastern shore, pass the campground and picnic area before returning to the ranger station.
- Jeffrey Pine Grove has young evergreens lining the trail that offer some welcome shade in warmer weather. Across the creek is a bench made from a tree.
- Chaos Crags and Jumbles was an enormous rock pile that collapsed cutting off a local stream and forming the lake.
- Popular for hiking, trail running, and fishing for rainbow and brown trout.
- Ride non-motorized boats or rent a kayak from the _Manzanita Lake camper store_ between 10 AM and 4 PM.
- Visit Loomis Museum (wheelchair accessible) to discover more about the park's history.

Sulphur Works

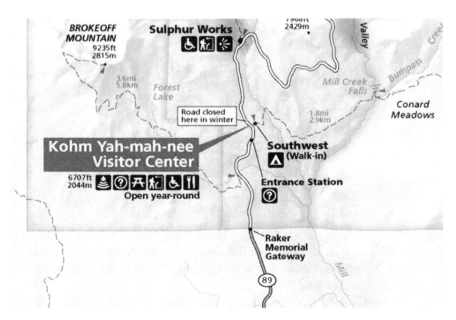

- The trailhead is 2 miles north of the southwest entrance near the Kohm Yah-mah-nee visitor center.
- 0.4 miles out-and-back, 46 feet elevation change, 10–15 minutes.
- Paved asphalt or concrete – wheelchair and stroller accessible.
- After a small loop past toilets, the trail follows the park's highway to an area that was once filled with a volcano.
- Volcanic sulfur bubbles span the whole area, which is impressive albeit smelly.
- Rest and enjoy a snack at picnic tables along the hike.
- Suitable for trail running.
- Popular for snowshoeing, especially after winter snowfall when roads may close.

Intermediate Trails

King's Creek Falls Trail

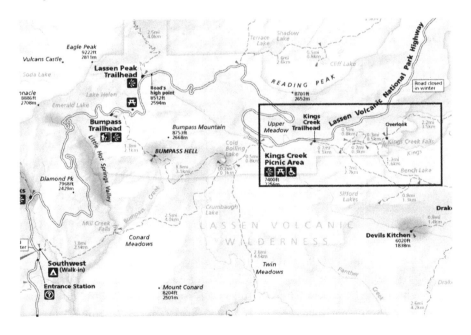

- The trailhead is in the middle of the park off the highway. Park off the road.
- 2.3-mile loop, 700 feet elevation change, 2 hours.

- The first part descends through meadows toward a creek that you will start following.
- At a junction 1 mile in, you can follow the steeper cascade trail or the horse trail, which is 0.3 miles longer but more gradual. Both paths join back at the creek and some smaller waterfalls.
- Next, you will reach the top of the falls before continuing around the trail to the view of the 40-foot waterfall from below.
- With caution, you can do some light scrambling to get closer to the falls.
- Some burnt landscape adds character and appreciation for the park's history.
- Ascending back along the creek is physically harder, but the views are more rewarding.
- This is a beautiful hike for wildflowers and animals, especially deer.

Devil's Kitchen Trail

Devils Kitchen Trail Map

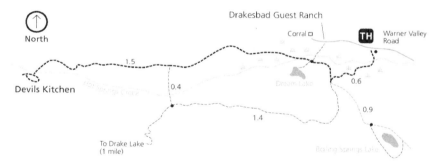

- The trailhead is off Chester-Warner Valley Road on a dirt road past the Warner Valley campground. Find limited parking here or turn right to the Devil's Kitchen picnic area for more.
- 4.2 miles out-and-back, 440 feet elevation change, 2–2.5 hours.
- When the road to the trailhead closes seasonally, add a few miles to the hike on snowshoes after snowfall.
- Begins with meadows, small footbridges, and boardwalks before an intersection. Stay right through another meadow.

- Follow Hot Springs Creek before a climb through the forest. The trail continues with some moderate ascents and descents followed by two stream crossings (depending on water levels) before a final hike up to the rim of Devil's Kitchen.
- From the rim, you can pass down 0.2 miles and cross Hot Springs Creek, which leads to red and yellow mounds in Devil's Kitchen. The name must come from the plopping and hissing emitted from the cracks in the ground and that potent sulphury smell.
- On the way back you can add 1 mile onto the hike by heading to Boiling Springs Lake.

Ridge Lakes Trail

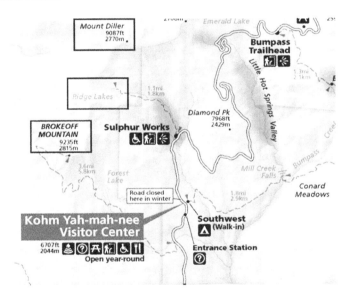

- The trailhead is in the Sulphur Works parking area on the north side next to the toilets.
- 2 miles out-and-back, 1,045 feet elevation change with heights of 7,000– 8,000 feet, 1.5–2 hours.
- Starts with an incline that gets steadily steeper.
- Several switchbacks wind throughout the forest before reaching a ravine up to the lake basin.
- This strenuous hike pays off when you are gazing over the two alpine lakes nestled between Mount Diller and Mount Brokeoff.

- Special wildflowers to look out for include mule's ear, Indian paintbrush, and lupine.
- It's likely that you will see frogs, deer, and black bears.
- Popular trail for skiing and snowshoeing in winter.

Advanced Trails

Lassen Peak

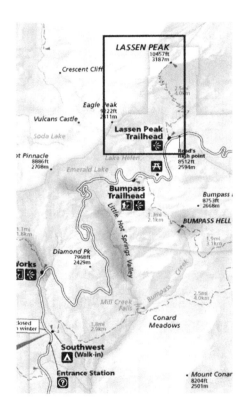

- Trailhead parking is 7 miles from the southwest entrance.
- 5 miles out-and-back, 1,957 feet elevation change, 4–5 hours.
- The trail heads north, then south briefly, and finally northeast. The incline begins as soon as the trees start to become sparser.
- At the beginning, look out for the Vulcan Eye carved into a distant rock.
- The challenging switchbacks take you to Lassen Peak's summit. Reaching the true summit may require some scrambling.

- Lassen Peak is one of the largest dome volcanoes in the world, and you can descend into the crater to explore the eruptions' remains. The trailhead starts at 8,500 feet and ascends to the park's tallest peak at 10,457 feet.
- With 360° views, the peak makes the perfect photo op or resting spot for a snack.
- Wildlife and wildflowers are plentiful along the way.
- You can often ski Lassen Peak from winter to spring.

Cinder Cone Trail

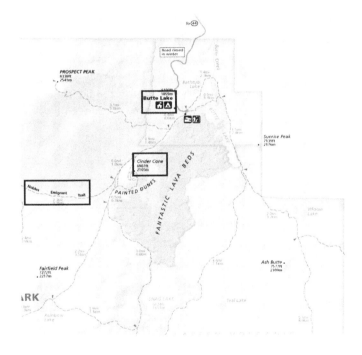

- Drive 24 miles from the northwest entrance toward the park's northeast corner to the Butte Lake parking lot. The trailhead is accessible via the 6-mile Butte Lake Road dirt road off Highway 44.
- 2.4 miles out-and-back to the base/4 miles out-and-back to the summit, 846 feet elevation change, 3–4 hours.
- Take sunglasses to protect your eyes from the dust on the trail.
- There are toilets at the trailhead and water at Butte Lake campground when it's open. Fill up here because there is little shade

on Cinder Cone. Also, take advantage of the Jeffrey pines at the base for a rest and some shade.

- Hiking over the cinders takes a bit more exertion, especially when climbing 200 feet up to the summit.
- Follow the path for 1.2 miles to the base before the trail starts to circle the south side of the Cinder Cone to the summit.
- At the summit, you can take another trail into the crater to explore.
- An alternative route takes the eastern path up the north side and loops the summit to join the trail on the south side to descend.
- Views include the Painted Dunes, and at the summit, you can take in 360° views of Lassen Peak, Prospect Peak, Snag Lake, and the Fantastic Lava Beds.
- Some of the Cinder Cones trail follows the Nobles Emigrant trail, part of the California National Historic trail. Read more information on the educational boards in the area.
- Stop off at the lake for a swim or non-motorized boating.
- Despite the landscape, there is still a surprising range of wildlife.

Brokeoff Mountain

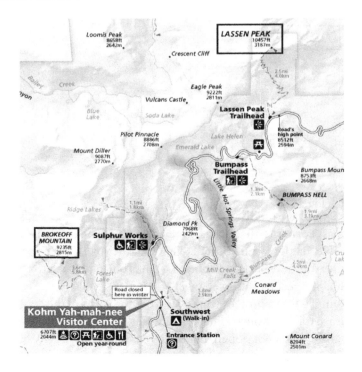

- The trailhead is across the road from the Brokeoff Mountain parking area near the southwest entrance.
- 7.4 miles out-and-back, 2,562 feet elevation change, 6 hours.
- The closest amenities, including toilets, are at the Kohm Yah-mah-nee visitor center.
- Starts with a narrow track through dense vegetation, woods, and then a marshy area. Past the marshy area, the mountain comes into view.
- There are a few switchbacks before following the trail up the side of the mountain. A final, large switchback from north to south will take you to the peak of the mountain.
- Brokeoff Mountain is an eroded stratovolcano formed when lava flow got stuck in the crater, which is what made the sides so steep.
- On your way up the mountain, note the impressive number of cinder cones you can see to the west.
- It's the second largest peak in Lassen Park at 9,235 feet. Aside from a panoramic view of the park, Brokeoff Mountain offers the best views of Lassen Peak to the northeast.
- Because it is less popular than the Lassen Peak trail, you may find total solace, especially early in the morning.

While Lassen Park is stunning and intriguing, it's essential to stay on the trails because straying not only disturbs the natural area but can be dangerous. Bumpass isn't the only person who has wandered off a trail and put their foot through the surface to burn parts of their body! This park is totally safe if you exercise care and remember that, unlike other parks, you can't explore freely here.

If you haven't had your share of volcanic activity, we are off to central California and Pinnacles National Park.

CHAPTER 10: PINNACLES NATIONAL PARK

"When we think of bees, what often comes to mind are honeybees or bumblebees, but these represent less than two percent of the nearly 500 bee species found at Pinnacles National Park. Bee diversity at Pinnacles ranks among the highest known anywhere on Earth."

— NATIONAL PARK SERVICE

CONTACT INFORMATION

Website: *General Information*

Phone Number: 831-389-4486

Address: 5000 Highway 146, Paicines, CA 95043

PARK OVERVIEW

Pinnacles National Park is a younger park after President Obama established the national monument as a national park in 2013. The park encom-
passes the remains of an ancient volcanic eruption 23 million years ago.
The 26,600 acres are split into the east and west with 30 miles of trails
joining them.

The park is full of admirable rock formations, huge monoliths, dramatic canyons, spires, and talus passages, all set in a canyon landscape. The park is known for its chaparral, oak woodlands, and caves. With such a stunning range of wildflowers, this park is home to 400 bee species.

It is also home to 48 types of mammals. Some of the most frequently spotted are black–tailed deer, bobcats, gray foxes, and raccoons. There are also brush rabbits, squirrels, chipmunks, and various bat species. Unlike other areas of Central California, this park has many reptiles from lizards to snakes. On that note, keep your eyes peeled for rattlesnakes! As for birds, you can find everything from hummingbirds to condors.

PLANNING

There are hikes that can be done quickly within a day, but to fully appreciate the park's grandeur, 2 days are best. While all campgrounds require reservations, entrance to the park does not.

Ideal times to visit are from mid-February to early June. Spring temperatures are mild hovering around 60–65°F. Toward May and June, they rise to around 78°F. Summer is not peak season because the temperatures can soar into the 90s°F drawing fewer crowds. Nighttime temperatures can drop to the 20s in winter with average daytime temperatures between 40–60°F. Despite the lower chance of snow at lesser elevations, this season still draws fewer crowds.

Cell service won't work in the park. While there is no free Wi-Fi, you can purchase it from the Pinnacles visitor center or by calling the park campground at 831-200-1722.

Both the east and west sides of the park are open year-round, but only the east side is open 24 hours. The west side allows entry between 7:30 AM–8:00 PM, however, you can leave anytime because there are automatic gates. There are no roads joining the east and west sides of the park.

ADMISSION AND FEES

Fees & Passes

As will all the national parks, you can enter the park for free on the 5 National Park free dates or use your America the Beautiful Pass to enter. Check the conditions of your pass because some offer additional benefits such as camping discounts.

For 7-day passes, the fees are as follows:

- Vehicles – $30
- Motorcycles – $25
- Walk-in/Bicycles – $15
- Annual Passes – $55

DIRECTIONS

Flying:

- San Jose, California: *San Jose International Airport*

Driving:

There is no public transport to the park, so you will need to drive.

- From San Jose airport, rent a car and take U.S. 101 S and CA 25 to Pinnacles National Park. It's an 80-mile drive and should take around 1.5 hours.
- From San Francisco Bay to the east entrance, take Highway 101 through Gilroy to Highway 25 before turning west on Highway 146.
- From San Francisco Bay to the west entrance, take Highway 101 South, head to Soledad, and then take Highway 146 East. Follow this road for 14 miles but be careful because it turns into a single lane.
- Heading from the south up to the east entrance, take Highway 101 North to King City, leaving at 1st Street. 1st Street becomes Bitterwater Rd and intersects Highway 25. Follow Highway 25 for 15 miles before turning onto Highway 146.

ACCOMMODATIONS

Camping is available at the _Pinnacles campground_ year-round on the east side of the park with tent sites, group camping sites, and RV sites (most with hookups). There are community tables, barbecue pits, and coin-operated showers. You will find water throughout the campground, but even more exciting is the swimming pool open from April–September, weather permitting. Contact 831-200-1722 for camping or campground store questions.

While there are no hotels in the park, there are canvas-sided tent cabins that are roomy enough for 4 people. Rent your tent cabin through _Pinnacles Recreation Company_ or _Recreation.gov_, or call 877-444-6777. Tent and RV sites can be booked up to 6 months in advance while group sites can be booked up to 12 months in advance.

Leashed dogs are welcome at the campground but aren't allowed on the trails.

PARK ATTRACTIONS

- _Bear Gulch nature center_: This is a must do before heading out on the hikes. There are exhibits, a video, and very knowledgeable rangers.
- Rock climbing: There are _climbs_ for all abilities on both the east and west sides. You can climb year-round except for summer when it's too hot. Climbing in Pinnacles is interesting because the rocks are volcanic breccia, which can break away unlike granite.
- _Bird watching_: The diverse terrain attracts an equally diverse range of birds– 160 species have been documented. Pine and oak trees are home to acorn woodpeckers, Steller's jays, black–headed grosbeaks, and warbling vireos. You may also see turkey vultures and golden eagles. A real treat is spotting the endangered California condor with its 9.5-foot-long wingspan; before captive breeding, there were only 25 condors left: _more bird watching_.

- *Talus caves*: These have openings that are formed by piles of boulders on a mountain slope. The park has 2 talus caves, Bear Gulch and Balconies, which are home to bat colonies and may be closed when bats are giving birth and raising their pups.

TOP HIKING TRAILS – LOCATIONS, SPECIFICATIONS, ACTIVITIES AND SITES

Beginner Trails

Bear Gulch Cave Trail – East Side

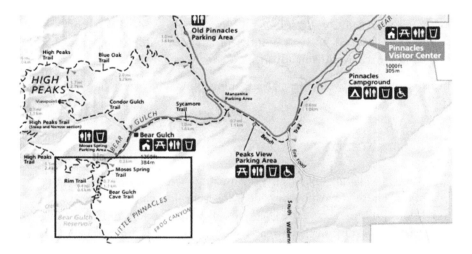

- The trail begins at the Bear Gulch day use area parking lot. There are toilets at the Pinnacles visitor center.
- 2.2 miles out-and-back (including the Moses Spring connector trail to the trailhead), 240 feet elevation change, 2 hours.
- Fun for surefooted children.
- The cave is closed from mid-May to mid-June.
- Be sure to take flashlights and a first aid kit just in case. Wear rain boots to avoid wet feet as there can be puddles throughout.
- The beginning of the trail passes under boulders and mini caves.
- The cave entrance begins wide but narrows as you progress with some areas requiring bending down low. White arrows on the floor provide guidance.

- Turn around and return the same way or join the cave loop back to the parking lot.
- Awesome bat cave experience with Towsend's big eared bats being one of the 16 bat species that live here.
- Wildflowers are predominant in spring and fall.
- At the end of the cave, there is a long set of steps that take you to views of Bear Gulch Reservoir surrounded by rock formations and trees.

Prewett Point Trail – West Side

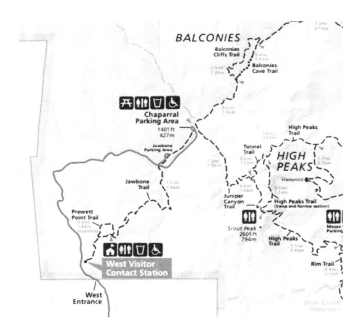

- Opening in 2019, this is the newest park trail located by the West visitor contact station parking lot where there are toilets.
- 0.9-mile lollipop loop, 78 feet elevation change, 15–20 minutes.
- Wheelchair and stroller accessible.
- Heads out through a large field with a gentle ascent as High Peaks and the fire tower on North Chalone Peak come into view.
- At the junction, keep right. The trail narrows as it goes around the hillside before joining back to the path to the parking lot.
- In the field look out for a sign about the Lyons family who were homesteaders in the area.

- There are pullouts and benches to stop and soak in the views of High Peaks and Balconies Cliffs where you may even see condors flying above.
- In the mornings and evenings, you might spot deer, turkeys, and turkey vultures.
- Suitable for trail running.

Jawbone Trail – West Side

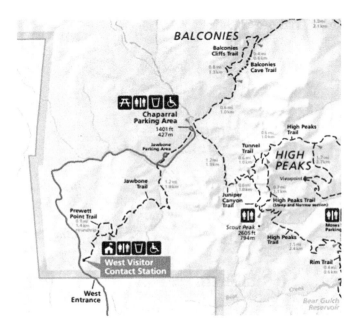

- Also a newer trail opened in spring 2017 that branches off Prewett Point trail after a 1/3rd of a mile in as indicated by a small sign. Or drive past the visitor center to the Jawbone parking area and start there.
- 2.4 miles out-and-back (from Jawbone parking lot around Prewitt Point trail), 560 feet elevation change, 30 minutes–1 hour.
- Narrow dirt trail – suitable for children.
- Descends and narrows to a single track wrapping around the hillside. Around the 0.8-mile mark, cross a wooden footbridge following the West Fork Chalone Creek. Past the bridge is the first viewpoint of the diverse chaparral ecosystem with broad leaved evergreens, shrubs, and small trees.

- The trail continues with some steps down to the Chaparral parking area where there are toilets and a picnic area.
- Lovely area for birdwatching and finding some peaceful solitude.
- Suitable for trail running.

Intermediate Trails

Moses Spring and Rim Trail Loop – East Side

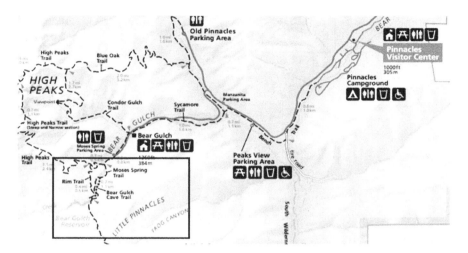

- Drive from the east entrance past the visitor center to the Bear Gulch day use area parking lot with toilets and picnic tables.
- 2.2-mile loop, 500 feet elevation change, 1–1.5 hours.
- Suitable for children.
- Don't forget the flashlight and first aid kit.
- Travels through Bear Gulch Cave, past the reservoir, and onto Rim trail before looping back to Moses Spring trail and then the parking lot.
- Admire views of the pinnacle rock formations, caves, forest, waterfalls, and the reservoir.
- Ideal for birdwatching and rock climbing.

Balconies Cave Trail – West Side

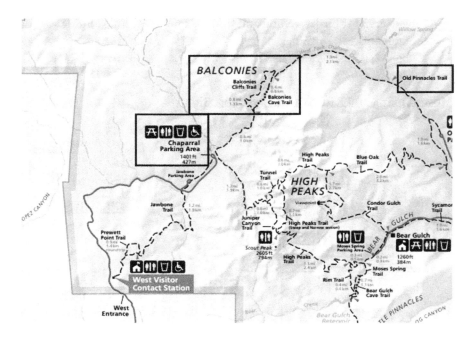

- Drive from the west entrance past the West visitor contact station to the Chaparral parking area with toilets and picnic tables.
- 2.4-mile lollipop loop, 100 feet elevation change, 1–1.5 hours.
- Bring a flashlight along with the right shoes for potential wet and slippery conditions in the cave. Wading may even be necessary during winter flooding.
- Head northeast along a sandy track down a slight descent into a canyon. Stop off at Machete Ridge before descending for some rock climbing.
- Follow the bottom of the canyon and then cross a footbridge. At the junction, head to the left to hike up and over Balconies Cave cliff.
- After the cliff, join the Old Pinnacles trail to travel back down through the cave and scramble through the talus passages (openings between boulders).
- Balconies Cave is split into two chambers. Pass through low ceilings and squeeze past boulders before a splash of daylight and then enter the second chamber.

Advanced Trails

Condor Gulch Trail to High Peaks Trail Loop – East Side

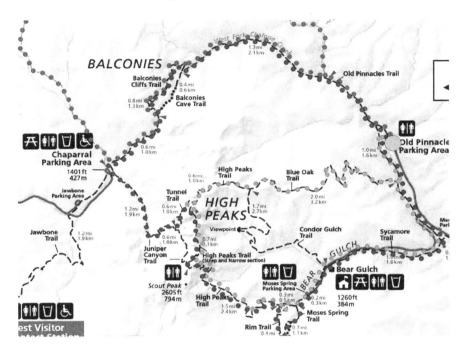

- Drive from the east entrance past the east visitor center to the Bear Gulch day use area parking lot with toilets and picnic tables. Alternatively, if parking is limited you can come in from the Chaparral parking area heading east along the High Peaks trail to join this loop.
- 5.3-mile loop, 1,300 feet elevation change, 3–5 hours.
- 3 miles into the hike is a toilet by a junction.
- Follow the Condor Gulch trail toward High Peaks crossing a short bridge before climbing up along the hillside and then curving to the left along a chalky trail up to the ridgeline.
- The first point of interest is the view of High Peaks, an interesting amphitheater of rocks seen from Condor Gulch Overlook.
- Other views include Bear Valley and the tip of Chalone Peak.
- Gorgeous scenery through the "steep and narrow section" of High Peaks trail that takes you right through the center of the Pinnacle rock formations.

- By the time you reach the High Peaks trail most of the elevation has been reached, so the hike back to the trailhead is a gentle one.
- It is beautiful year-round, especially in spring when the flowers bloom.
- Parts of the trail are suitable for trail running, and other parts may require some scrambling.
- Extend the loop to 6.1 miles by adding the Rim and Moses Spring trails.

High Peaks to Balconies Cave Loop Trail – West or East Side

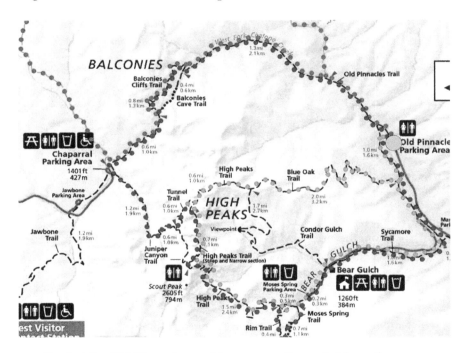

- Start at the Old Pinnacles parking area on the east side or the Chaparral parking area on the west.
- 8.4-mile loop, 1,540 feet elevation change, 5 hours.
- The route is well signed with several toilets along the loop.
- From the Old Pinnacles trailhead, hike the most challenging part up to High Peaks before joining the Tunnel trail followed by Juniper Canyon trail.

- Next, the trail passes the Chaparral picnic area. From here, take the Balconies Cave trail through the cave and back to Old Pinnacles trail.
- Enjoy some of the best park features from pinnacle views to cave adventures.
- Look out for wildlife including condors, reptiles, deer, bobcats, and wild turkeys. You may also see wildflowers like Milk Maidens and Indian Paintbrushes.
- Some parts are suitable for trail running, and other rocky parts offer scrambling opportunities.
- Stop off for lunch at the Chaparral picnic area to recharge your batteries before exploring the cave. Don't forget your flashlight and sturdy shoes!

Juniper Canyon Trail to High Peaks – West Side

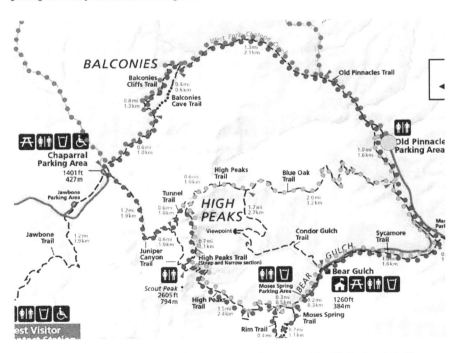

- Park in the Chaparral parking area on the west side. If the lot is full, utilize the Jawbone parking area adding an extra 0.5 miles to the hike.
- 4.3-mile loop, 1,215 feet elevation change, 2.5–3 hours.

- Juniper Canyon trail bears right at the first junction passing a creek bed that is normally dry before entering the canyon.
- Travel through trees and a rock jumble followed by a streambed and waterway before an incline and several switchbacks as you ascend. At the top, you will reach "Comfort Station," a bench to enjoy Saddle Junction and High Peaks.
- The trail over High Peaks traverses several staircases (built by the Civilian Conservation Corps back in 1933), more switchbacks, and a tunnel before joining back onto the Juniper Canyon trail. Humans carved the 120-foot tunnel through a solid rock buttress.
- Marvel at various trees from oaks to cottonwoods, buckeyes, and gray pines, as well as bright wildflowers.
- Keep an eye out for Resurrection Wall, Machete Ridge, and Bear Valley. Enjoy the thrill of fissures and near vertical drops to the gulch below.

2 things I love about Pinnacles National Park are the reduced crowds and how the trails are all conveniently linked. No road connecting the east to the west side keeps the center of the park cleaner and quieter. If you time it just right, it's possible to not see a single other person on certain trails offering a true escape from society.

* * *

Next we are off to a park that is named after the trees but has much more than just some of the tallest trees in the world.

CHAPTER 11: REDWOOD NATIONAL AND STATE PARKS

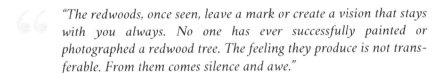

"The redwoods, once seen, leave a mark or create a vision that stays with you always. No one has ever successfully painted or photographed a redwood tree. The feeling they produce is not transferable. From them comes silence and awe."

— *JOHN STEINBECK*

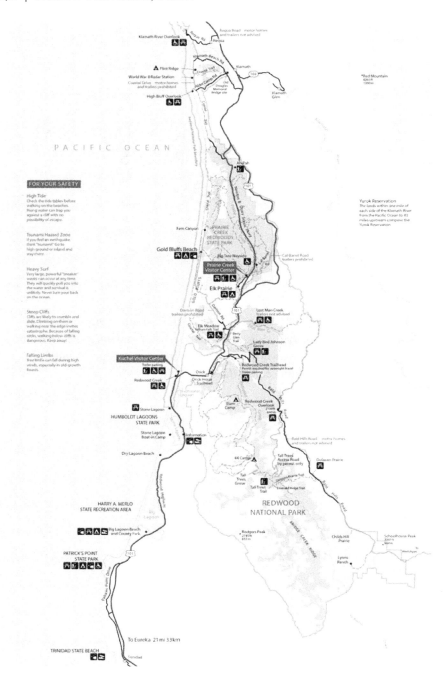

CONTACT INFORMATION

- Website: *General Information*
- Phone Number: 707-464-6101
- Address: 1111 Second Street, Crescent City, CA 95531 (Headquarters)

PARK OVERVIEW

Where north California meets the shore you will find Redwood National Park, a World Heritage Site and International Biosphere Reserve. The park is 131,983 acres boasting 200 miles of trails. It was established as a national park in 1968. You can visit the park year-round and it's open 24 hours a day.

The redwoods here are some of the tallest and oldest in the world. Ponder that some of the trees date back to before the Roman Empire and reach 370 feet, which is 5 stories higher than the Statue of Liberty!

There are actually 4 parks in 1. Redwoods National Park is joined by Jedediah Smith Redwoods State Park, Del Norte Coast Redwoods State Park, and Prairie Creek Redwoods State Park. There is even more diversity than other parks with prairies, rivers, streams, forests, and lagoons, plus 37 miles of pristine coastline.

PLANNING

In 2 days, you will have enough time to complete several shorter hikes, but because of the acreage spread across 4 parks, 3 days or more are better.

Summer is peak session attracting more crowds. While summer temperatures can reach the upper 60s°F, they average in the upper 50s°F. Average lows in the winter are around 40°F with a greater chance of rain. Of course, it can rain at any time of year, so it's worth packing raincoats. Spring and fall offer beautiful weather. Travel here between December–April if you hope to catch a glimpse of gray whales migrating.

Cell coverage is very limited around the parks. Your best chance of coverage is around Crescent City, Hiouchi visitor center, Prairie Creek visitor center, and the southern end of Newton B. Drury Scenic Parkway. There is some coverage at the Jedediah Smith Redwoods campground, too.

ADMISSION AND FEES

Fees & Passes

While there are no fees to enter Redwood National and State Parks, there are day fees for some areas. For the Gold Bluffs Beach/Fern Canyon area, it costs $12, and for the Jedediah Smith Campground, the day fee is $8. If you have an America the Beautiful Pass, these fees are waived. They are also waived on the 5 days where there are no National Park fees. Pay for the day entrances at the entrance stations to the developed campgrounds.

DIRECTIONS

Conveniently, there are various ways to reach the parks.

Flying:

- Crescent City, California: *Del Norte County Airport*
- Medford, Oregon: *Rogue Valley International-Medford Airport* (100 miles from Hiouchi visitor center)
- McKinleyville, California: *Humboldt County Airport* (25 miles from Kuchel visitor center)

Driving:

This is the first park where GPS navigates correctly if you enter one of the visitor center addresses.

- Humboldt Redwoods State Park Interpretive & Visitor Center– 17119 Avenue of the Giants, Weott 95573
- Redwood National & State Park Visitor Center (Thomas H. Kuchel Visitor Center) – 11944 Hwy 101, Orick, CA 95555

Public Transport:

There is a bus route with service between Crescent City, Smith River, Gasquet, Klamath, Orick, and Arcata. Obtain more information about their routes through the website _Redwood Coast transit_ or by calling 707-464-6400. Those under 18 years old and veterans travel for free.

Redwood Adventures shuttle services operates large vans out of Orick, California that offer several one-way adventure shuttles or even custom shuttle routes. Routes can be booked online in advance or by calling 707-727-9266.

ACCOMMODATIONS

There are no hotels inside the parks, but there are 8 cabins, 4 in Elk Prairie campground and 4 in the Jedediah Smith Redwoods State Park. These cabins are often booked 6 months in advance.

There are 4 _campgrounds_ across the parks where you need to make reservations at least 48 hours in advance at _ReserveCalifornia_ or call 800-400-7275. The standard fee is $35 per night, but those with an America the Beautiful Pass receive a discount. If you are traveling by RV, check with the campsite if there is a size restriction.

- Jedediah Smith – 10 miles east of Crescent City on Highway 199 with 86 sites, hot showers, ADA accessible restrooms, picnic tables, fire pits and barbeques, and food lockers.
- Mill Creek – 7 miles south of Crescent City on Highway 101 with 145 sites, hot showers, ADA accessible restrooms, picnic tables, fire pits and barbeques, and food lockers.
- Elk Prairie – 6 miles north of Orick on the Newton B. Drury Scenic Parkway with 75 sites, hot showers, ADA accessible restrooms, picnic tables, fire pits and barbeques, and food lockers.
- Gold Bluffs Beach – 10 miles north of Orick on Davison Road (no trailers) with 26 sites, solar showers, restrooms, wind shelters, picnic tables, fire pits and barbeques, and food lockers.

Backcountry camping is available at 7 sites, all of which require a free permit that must be reserved online: _backcountry permits_.

- Little Bald Hills
- DeMartin
- Flint Ridge
- Gold Bluffs Beach
- Elam Camp
- 44 Camp
- Redwood Creek Dispersed

Pets are only allowed at the developed campgrounds, but you can also take your leashed dog to the beaches, picnic areas, and roads. They aren't allowed on the trails.

PARK ATTRACTIONS

- Gold Bluffs Beach: This area gets its name from the legendary golden colored bluffs. The miles of gray sand and protected dunes are great places for camping. There is a good chance of seeing an elk herd pop by as well as seals, sea birds, and migrating whales and dolphins.
- Avenue of the Giants: Located in Humboldt Redwoods State Park, this has been called one of the finest forest drives in the world and consists of 31 miles lined by titan trees. There is a great photo opportunity where the road is split by a giant tree that you can pass through.
- Redwood Creek Overlook: Great spot for a picturesque sunset. At 1,000 feet above the ocean, the overlook allows you to watch the clouds sweep below you as the sun sets over the treetops.
- Tall Trees Grove: This is home to Libbey Tree, which was once the tallest living thing in the park. It's actually the only one of the former Tallest Trees that you can still see. A free pass is required to access this area: _Tall Trees Grove permit_.
- Elk Meadow: This is the place to spot Roosevelt Elk, as well as other wildlife. Close by is Prairie Creek, a chance to spot salmon and other fish. It's a popular area for biking and a good starting point for many hikes.

- *Fishing*: Catch salmon and trout in the Smith and Klamath rivers, trout in Redwood Creek, or night smelt and surfperch along park beaches. You must have a California state fish license and should consult fishing regulations at any park visitor center, call 707-445-6493, or check *California Department of Fish and Wildlife*.
- Horseback Riding: There are several designated *pack animal trails and overnight camps* (free permit required).
- *Cycling*: Bicycles, mountain bikes, and e-bikes are permitted on several trails. Elk Meadow day use area connects different bike trails in Greater Prairie Creek watershed.

TOP HIKING TRAILS – LOCATIONS, SPECIFICATIONS, ACTIVITIES AND SITES

Beginner Trails

Lady Bird Johnson Grove Trail – South

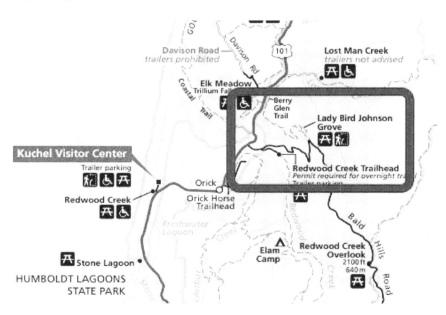

- Highway 101 traverses the park from north to south. Bald Hills Road forks off from it near Kuchel visitor center in the southern half of the park. The parking lot is 3 miles from this junction up

Bald Hill Road in the Prairie Creek Redwoods. Do not park on the road.

- 3-mile lollipop loop, 101 feet elevation change, 30 minutes.
- Wheelchair and stroller accessible, although help may be needed over the bridge.
- Head out early in the morning to avoid crowds.
- In summer, there are ranger led walks to learn park information.
- Several informational plaques guide the way, plus there is a dedication plaque for Lady Bird Johnson, President Nixon's wife.
- After crossing the bridge, turn left or right at a junction onto the loop.
- At over 1,000 feet above sea level, this leaves behind the noise pollution from roads.
- Though the views aren't extensive, the redwoods are amazing especially because they have never been logged. Often there is fog that adds to the trail's beauty.

Yurok Loop Trail – North

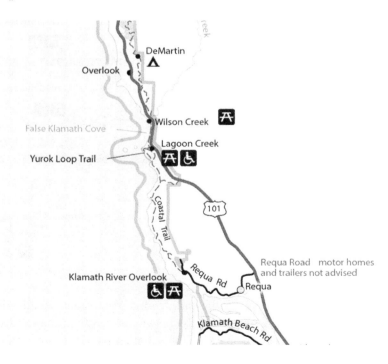

- The trailhead is off Highway 101 at the Lagoon Creek picnic area with a parking lot and toilets.
- 1-mile loop, 100 feet elevation change, 30 minutes.
- Wheelchair and stroller accessible.
- Head northwest to an intersection where you can turn right or left to take the loop in either direction.
- Heading right/north, you have views of False Klamath Cove. As you curve around the west side, you will see millions of seabirds roosting on sea stacks (rock columns) near the shore.
- Hike through wildflowers and a coastal forest densely populated with fir and spruce trees before looping around past Lagoon Pond.
- At the side trail to Wilson Beach is a driftwood strewn cove.
- Extend the hike from the south part of the loop 4 miles down to Klamath River overlook.

Ah-Pah Interpretive Trail – South

- The trailhead is at the north end of Newton B. Drury Scenic Parkway with room for a few cars off the road.
- 0.6 miles out-and-back, 6 feet minimal elevation change, 15–20 minutes.

- Wheelchair and stroller accessible.
- Head east into a redwood grove with a natural arch covered in vibrant vegetation. Close by is an unofficial trail to a ravine.
- Informational plaques along the trail explain the park's logging history and highlight the successful forest restoration on this trail.
- Suitable for trail running.

Intermediate Trails

Tall Trees Grove Loop Trail – South

- The trailhead is 7 miles along Bald Hills Road where it branches from Highway 101. Entry into Tall Trees Grove is limited to 50 cars per day. Apply for a *permit* online to receive an emailed access code to get into the gate. Because of the narrow roads and small parking lot, no vehicles over 21 feet are permitted.
- 4.5-mile lollipop loop, 1,600 feet elevation change, 2–2.5 hours. Allow an additional 2 hours of driving time to and from the trailhead.

- Take food, water, a raincoat, and a flashlight since this hike is remote with less foot traffic, which allows you to enjoy complete tranquility surrounded by nature.
- Hike about 1.5 miles to the short 1-mile loop followed by the same 1.5-mile route back. The return can be strenuous with several inclines.
- There are 2 streams to cross with footbridges available during summer. Take care when crossing as high water can be dangerous.
- The loop passes Redwood River, a perfect spot to relax.
- The giant redwoods are widely spaced with 5-foot ferns, hazelnut trees, and other small trees in between offering unique photo opportunities.
- Look out for the massive fallen tree you can walk through and the magnificent, twisted California Bay tree.
- You are likely to see wildlife, especially deer.

Trillium Falls Trail – South

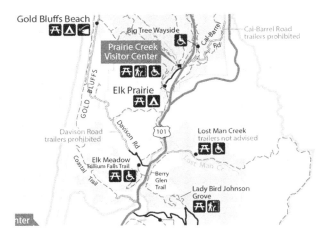

- The trailhead is well marked off Highway 101 near the Elk Meadow day use area with plenty of parking.
- 2.8-mile loop, 440 feet elevation change, 1–1.5 hours.
- Mainly paved trail – suitable for older children.
- Take the paved access path toward Davison Road before heading right onto Trillium Falls trail. There are a few switchbacks and then a metal footbridge to cross.
- The final 1.3 miles takes you north to a dirt logging road.

- Trillium Falls is a stunning waterfall and a chance to snap some photos. There is a viewing point, but don't be tempted to exit the trail.
- Diverse vegetation includes Western trillium, giant trillium, old growth redwoods, blackberry brambles, huckleberry shrubs, ferns, and maples, to name a few.
- Keep your eyes peeled for an elk herd.

Redwood Creek Trail – South

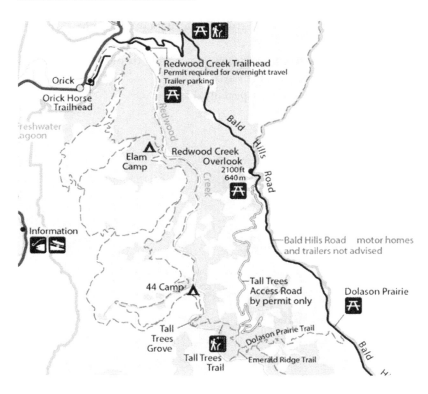

- Take Bald Hills Road for 0.5 miles to a parking area by the trailhead.
- 15.4 miles out-and-back, 500 feet elevation change, 7–8 hours.
- Suitable for older children.
- 1.5 miles into the hike is the first of 2 creek crossings. There are footbridges during summer only, and extreme caution should be exercised when crossing the creeks without these footbridges.

- After the first creek crossing, the trail becomes less maintained but is marked with orange signs. Next, you will head toward Elam Camp.
- After crossing the second dramatic footbridge, the trail has some ups and downs toward 44 Camp (where you can stay overnight) and then on to Tall Trees loop. You can add this 1-mile loop or turn around and head back.
- There are old and second growth redwoods, Douglas Firs, salmonberry, blackberry, and maples, plus dozens of different wildflowers in spring.
- The creeks are idyllic where you can relax while taking in the views or fishing. You can also backcountry camp along the banks.

Advanced Trails

Mill Creek Horse Trail – North

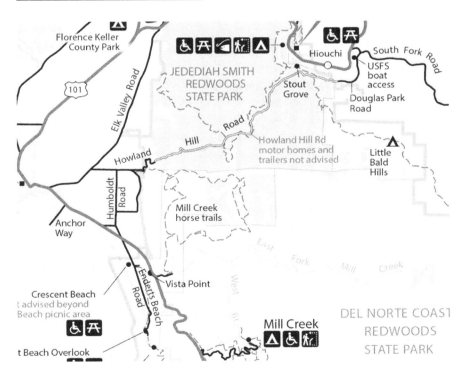

The trailhead is found at the parking lot off Bertsch Street via Howland Hill Road.

then passes Mill Creek Watershed's hills and is marked with
wooden signs from this point on.

- From the trailhead, it is 4.8 miles to the park's boundary followed
  by 5 additional miles on Paradise Flat trail through Smith River
  National Recreation Area.
- Follow the Smith's River south fork through a diverse range of
  prairies and forests, each containing various trees, plants, and
  flowers that change along the trail. Look out for Douglas fir,
  coffeeberry shrubs, huckleberry shrubs, and azalea flowers, to name
  a few.
- This is a lovely escape from crowds.
- Suitable for mountain biking and horseback riding.

The final park is one that might be one of the best known, but there is still
plenty to discover.

CHAPTER 12: YOSEMITE NATIONAL PARK

"This one noble park is big enough and rich enough for a whole life of study and aesthetic enjoyment. It is good for everybody, no matter how benumbed with care, encrusted with a mail of business habits like a tree with bark. None can escape its charms. Its natural beauty cleans and warms like a fire, and you will be willing to stay forever in one place like a tree."

— *JOHN MUIR*

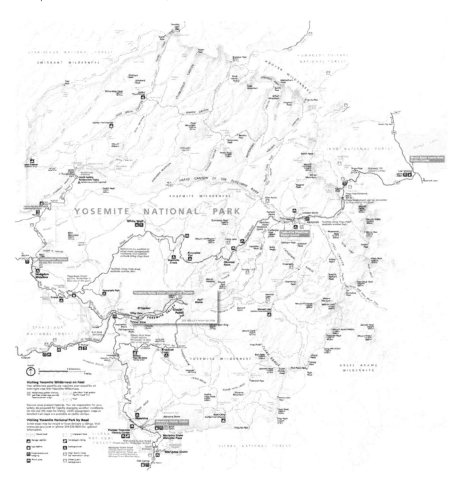

CONTACT INFORMATION

Website: *General Information*

Phone Number: 209-372-0200

Address: Tioga Road Highway 120 & Highway 140, CA 95389

PARK OVERVIEW

Yosemite National Park is in the western Sierra Nevada Mountain range. It covers over 1,200 square miles making it one of the largest national parks. In 1864 President Lincoln signed the Yosemite Land Grant protecting

Mariposa Grove and Yosemite Valley. John Muir campaigned for the park to be established as a national park, and President Benjamin Harrison signed the law in 1890. Because Yosemite is home to sacred ancient homelands of American Indian Tribes and their traditions, it is a UNESCO World Heritage Site.

Yosemite is known for its stunning natural beauty including towering granite cliffs, cascading waterfalls, pristine lakes, and giant sequoia trees. Yosemite Valley is ½ mile deep and 7 miles wide. Millions of years of glaciation resulted in a diverse topography with 800 miles of hiking trails.

California is home to 7,000 plant species, 50% of which are in the Sierra Nevada. Yosemite is home to over 20% of those plants with 160 species being unique to the park. The park is also home to a diverse array of wildlife with 400 vertebrates including black bears, mountain lions, bobcats, coyotes, mule deer, and many bird species.

PLANNING

1 day would be enough for a good hike and to experience some other key attractions by car. 3 days is ideal, but avid hikers could easily spend 5 days exploring the park.

The park attracts almost 4 million visitors annually with July and August being the most popular. The expansive area with varied elevations leads to variable weather throughout the park. Valley temperatures in summer range from 57–89°F whereas winter can drop as low as 28–48°F. May, June, September, and October are the ideal months for fewer crowds and enjoyable hiking weather. 75% of rain and snow precipitation occurs between November and March.

Those staying at Ahwahnee Hotel, Yosemite Valley Lodge, Curry Village, and Wawona Hotel have internet access, and there is Wi-Fi available at Mariposa County libraries in Yosemite Valley and Wawona as well as Deganan's Kitchen. Cell service is not always reliable. You are more likely to have cell service in the eastern part of the valley, but I wouldn't bet on this.

ADMISSION AND FEES

Fees & Passes

Yosemite National Park offers 5 free national park days and accepts America the Beautiful passes. The park is free for 4th graders and their families, U.S. military personnel and their dependents, and U.S. citizens or permanent residents with permanent disabilities. Other fees include:

- 7-day vehicle – $35
- Motorcycle – $30
- Foot/bike/horse – $20
- Annual Pass – $80
- Lifetime senior pass – $80
- Annual senior pass – $20

You can pay in advance online or at any of the park entrances. All entrances are open 24 hours a day except Hetch Hetchy. If the entrance is unstaffed, you can pay on the way out. They accept cards and mobile payments but not cash.

DIRECTIONS

Reaching this very popular park is relatively straightforward.

Flying:

- Fresno, California: *Fresno Yosemite International Airport* is just 1.25 hours away from South entrance via Highway 41.
- San Francisco, California: *San Francisco International Airport* is 2.5 hours from the Big Oak Flat entrance when taking Highway 120.
- Mariposa, California: *Mariposa-Yosemite Airport* is only 30 minutes from the Arch Rock entrance via Highway 140.

Driving:

Bear in mind that the times above are to the respective entrances not Yosemite Valley. It will often take up to an hour from the entrance to the actual valley. There are 5 entrances to Yosemite National Park.

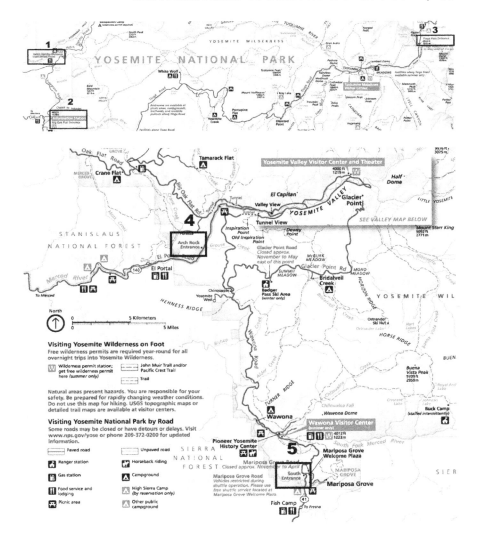

Visiting Yosemite Wilderness on Foot
Free wilderness permits are required year-round for all overnight trips into Yosemite Wilderness.

Wilderness permit station; get free wilderness permit here *(summer only)*	John Muir Trail and/or Pacific Crest Trail
	Trail

Natural areas present hazards. You are responsible for your safety. Be prepared for rapidly changing weather conditions. Do not use this map for hiking. USGS topographic maps or detailed trail maps are available at visitor centers.

Visiting Yosemite National Park by Road
Some roads may be closed or have detours or delays. Visit www.nps.gov/yose or phone 209-372-0200 for updated information.

Paved road	Unpaved road
Ranger station	Horseback riding
Gas station	Campground
Food service and lodging	High Sierra Camp *(by reservation only)*
Picnic area	Other public campground

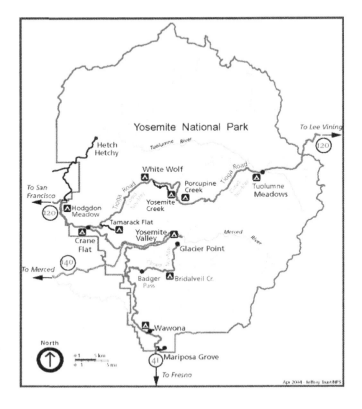

1. Hetch Hetchy: Take Highway 120 and Evergreen Road. Vehicles can't exceed 25 feet long, 8 feet wide, and 14 feet tall.
2. Big Oak Flat: Highway 120 East (Manteca) leads you here. You may need tire chains in winter. There is also a tunnel, so vehicles can't be taller than 13 feet 8 inches. If your vehicle is over 12 feet tall, you will need to exit from a different entrance as it won't fit back through the tunnel.
3. Tioga: Begin on U.S. 395 to Lee Vining gas station, then Highway 120 West to reach this entrance, which may be closed in winter due to snow.
4. Arch Rock: Accessible via Highway 140 East (Merced). There is also a chance tire chains are needed in winter, and there is a height restriction of 12 feet 10 inches.
5. South Entrance: Take Highway 41 North (Fresno) here. The height restrictions are 10 feet 2 inches entering and 13 feet 6 inches exiting.

Public transport:

Yarts bus service takes passengers to various visitor centers/trailheads and back. You can catch one of the buses year-round from the main station on Highway 140. Buses run in summer from Highway 120 East, Highway 120 North, and Highway 41 (Fresno). Tickets can be reserved and pre-purchased through their website.

ACCOMMODATIONS

There are dozens of options when planning your stay in Yosemite. Because of the numerous options it's advised to check with the specific accommodation to confirm booking and prices.

Lodging:

- Ahwahnee Hotel – Previously Majestic Yosemite Hotel, it is the only luxury hotel in Yosemite found in the valley and open year-round.
- Yosemite Valley Lodge – Located close to Yosemite Falls with a good restaurant and is also open year-round.
- Wawona Hotel – Previously Big Trees Lodge, it's a Victorian lodge close to Mariposa Grove and Giant Sequoias.
- Curry Village– Previously Half Dome Village, this is a group of canvas-sided tent cabins in the center of the valley.
- Housekeeping Camp – Open-air site in the valley close to Merced River.
- White Wolf Lodge – Canvas-sided tents 30 miles from the valley combining everyday luxuries with tranquility.
- Tuolumne Meadows Lodge – Canvas-tent cabins 8,700 feet above sea level with no electricity, but showers are available.
- High Sierra Camps – Lottery based booking with all the fun of backpacking without the need to lug tents or cooking equipment.
- Glacier Point Ski Hut – Sleeps up to 20 people, ideal for winter sports, views, and a handy bus service.

You can reserve lodgings along with guided bus tours, hikes, and backpacking through *travel Yosemite*.

Camping:

There are 13 campgrounds in Yosemite. Some are available on a first come first serve basis; others need to be booked 2 weeks, 2 months, or even 5 months in advance depending on the camp. Book through this *campgrounds* website or call 877-444-6777.

- Upper Pines – Open year-round, $36 per night, tap water, ADA accessible, reservations 5 months in advance.
- Lower Pines – Seasonal, $36 per night, tap water, ADA accessible, reservations 5 months in advance.
- North Pines – Seasonal, $36 per night, tap water, ADA accessible, reservations lottery or 5 months in advance.
- Camp 4 – Year-round, no RVs/trailers, $10 per night, tap water, ADA accessible, reservations 2 weeks ahead from May to October.
- Wawona – Year-round, $36 per night, tap water, ADA accessible, reservations 5 months ahead for April to October.
- Bridalveil Creek – Seasonal, $36 per night, tap water, reservations 2 months in advance.
- Hodgdon Meadow – Year-round, $36 per night, tap water, reservations 2 months ahead for April to October.
- Crane Flat – Seasonal, $36 per night, tap water, ADA–accessible, reservations 2 months ahead.
- Tamarack Flat – Seasonal, $24 per night, RVs/trailers not recommended, creek for water, ADA accessible, reservations 2 months and 2 weeks in advance
- White Wolf – Seasonal, $30 per night, tap water, reservations 2 months and 2 weeks ahead.
- Yosemite Creek – Seasonal, RVs/trailers not recommended, $24 per night, ADA accessible, creek for water, reservations 2 weeks ahead.
- Porcupine Flat – Seasonal, RVs/trailers not recommended, $24 per night, ADA accessible, creek for water, reservations 2 weeks ahead.
- Tuolumne Meadows – Currently closed, $36 per night, ADA accessible, tap water.

Act fast to get reservations when tickets are released at 7 AM Pacific time. Log into the website beforehand as reservations can sell out in a matter of minutes.

Pets aren't allowed in the lodging areas but can be taken to all the camp-grounds except the walk-in and group grounds (including Camp 4). Leashed pets are also welcome on paved roads and sidewalks but not on trails.

PARK ATTRACTIONS

- *Cycling*: Rent bikes, ADA bikes, and electric scooters from Curry Village, Yosemite Village, and Yosemite Valley Lodge. There is also a bike sharing program.
- Horseback riding: *Yosemite Trails horseback adventures* offers 1 and 2-hour rides and an exclusive day ride to Mariposa Grove. *Wawona Stables* rents mules and horses for their 2–hour and ½ day rides.
- *Yosemite museum*: Discover the first people who lived in the valley over 3,000 years ago with displays and well–informed staff to answer any questions.
- Rock climbing: As the most famous *rock climbing* destination in the U.S., Yosemite has attracted not only amateur climbers but also climbing legends over the decades. Camp 4 has been listed on the National Register of Historic Places because of its popularity with climbers.
- Auto Touring: There are many *scenic drives* through Yosemite but none more so than Tioga Road which takes you through alpine scenery, lakes, and wildflower filled meadows with elevations of 9,945 feet to Tioga Pass. Usually open late May–November.
- Bird watching: There are 165 species and up to 100 more migratory birds in the park. You may spot ravens, acorn woodpeckers, Steller's jay, and northern pygmy owls.
- Yosemite Falls: This 2,425-foot waterfall can be seen from various points in the park, and you can hike close enough to feel the mist on your face.
- Horsetail Falls: Typically flows only in winter but in mid to late February it can glow orange against the sunset in evenings with clear skies when water is flowing. Due to its popularity, restrictions apply from mid to late February each year so consult the website before traveling: *Horsetail Falls*.

- Happy Isles art and nature center: This *educational center* teaches about the ecosystem in the park through art workshops, interactive displays, and exhibits.
- *Fishing*: Streams and rivers have an abundance of fish, offering a thrilling and surreal experience set in such incredible scenery. A license is needed, and fishing regulations must be followed.

TOP HIKING TRAILS – LOCATIONS, SPECIFICATIONS, ACTIVITIES AND SITES

Beginner Trails

Lower Yosemite Falls – Yosemite Valley

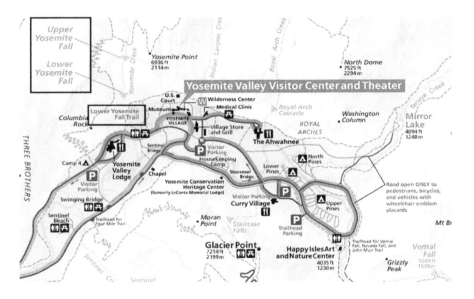

- The trailhead is off Northside Drive west of Yosemite Village where there is parking. There is also a wheelchair accessible shuttle, toilets, and a picnic area at the trailhead.
- 1.1-mile loop, 55 feet elevation change, 30 minutes.
- Paved or wooden boards – wheelchair and stroller accessible.
- After staying right at the intersection, the trail crosses Yosemite Creek before viewing the falls. It then heads north through a forest and curves southeast back toward the trailhead.

- There are several cascade viewpoints along the trail. The 320-foot drop of Lower Yosemite Falls is the third part of Yosemite Falls, and you get close enough to feel the mist.
- This short hike is packed with photo opportunities of the soaring cliffs, tree-lined corridors, and waterfalls.
- Don't be tempted to stray off the trail because the rocks can be slippery, or there may be some falling rocks.
- Watch out for deer herds.
- Reserve this hike for spring to see water since the falls can be dry in July and August.
- Expect icy conditions during winter.

Glacier Point Trail – Yosemite Valley

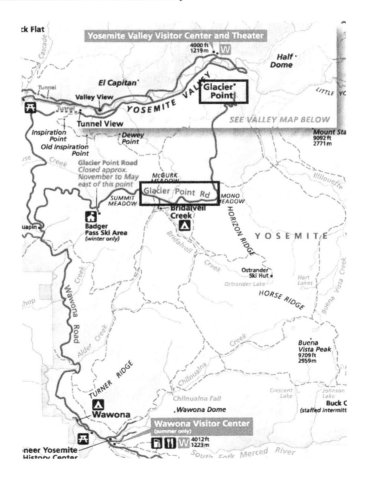

- The trail begins at the Glacier Point parking lot off Glacier Point Road, accessible via Wawona Road past the Wawona visitor center, close to South entrance.
- 0.6-mile elongated loop, 137 feet elevation change, 15–20 minutes.
- Paved – wheelchair and stroller accessible.
- Head straight out from the parking lot and keep to the right when the trail splits. As the path gently inclines, the trees thin to make way for the views.
- After reaching Glacier Point, you can return the same way or take a left toward the stone building, Glacier Point Trailside Museum, a historic building constructed in 1924 as one of the first projects in the park.
- Glacier Point towers above the valley at a whopping 7,214 feet offering one of the best views of Yosemite Valley in the park.
- Breathtaking 270° views of Lower and Upper Yosemite Falls, Clouds Rest, Half Dome, Vernal Falls, and Nevada Falls.
- Stop off at Glacier Point Gift Shop to pick up souvenirs and a snack. Near the gift shop is an amphitheater and fire pit where you can hear rangers talk about the history of this part of the park.

Sentinel and Cook's Meadow Loop Trail – Yosemite Valley

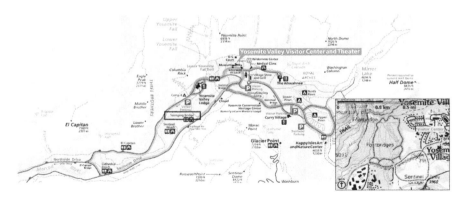

- Park at the sign for Swinging Bridge on Southside Drive. There is also ADA accessible parking on Northside Drive. There are toilets in the parking lot and along the trail.
- 2-mile loop, 77 feet elevation change, 1 hour.
- Partially paved – wheelchair and stroller accessible.

- Cook's Meadow is north of Merced River while Sentinel Meadow is south of the river.
- Swinging and Sentinel bridges offer great views of Yosemite Falls and Half Dome, respectively.
- Keep a lookout for Yosemite Chapel. Built in 1879, it is the oldest building in Yosemite.
- Spring is a beautiful time for wildflowers such as cow parsnip and western azalea blanketing the meadows. Stay on the path to not damage the delicate ecosystem.
- At Yosemite Lodge you can pick up a snack, visit one of the restaurants, or enjoy a drink at the bar.

Mirror Lake Trail – Yosemite Valley

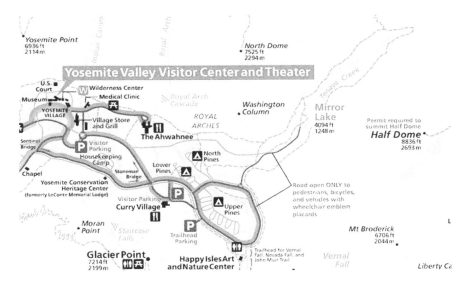

- There is no parking at the Mirror Lake Trailhead, so either park at Curry Village and walk or catch the shuttle to stop #17: *Yosemite shuttle*.
- 2 miles out-and-back, 100 feet elevation change, 1 hour.
- Paved – wheelchair and stroller accessible.
- The path leads straight to Mirror Lake, famous for the mountains reflecting off the water.
- By late summer the water recedes and is replaced by sand and grass being referenced as Mirror Meadow at this point. There are

informational plaques on the trail explaining the lake to meadow succession.

- This is a rare trial that allows leashed dogs; however, they are not allowed on the shuttle buses.
- There are toilets halfway along the trail.
- Lakeshore is a divine spot for a picnic or a refreshing swim in the lake.
- Backcountry camping is available, or you are close to Yosemite Village and Curry Village for lodging.
- Popular for hiking, biking, and trail running.
- At the end you can continue another 3-mile loop (5 miles, 2–3 hours total) around the lake, although this part of the trail isn't paved.
- The loop follows Tenaya Creek after the lake and crosses 2 bridges before returning past the lake to its south.

Intermediate Trails

Valley Loop Trail – Yosemite Valley

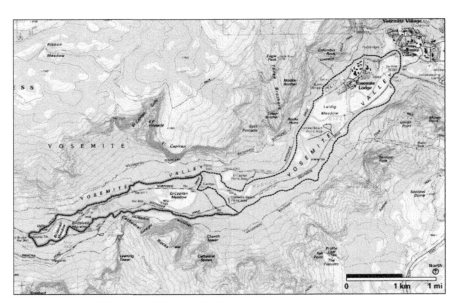

- Start at the Lower Yosemite Falls trailhead off Northside Drive west of Yosemite Village where there is parking. There is also a wheelchair accessible shuttle, toilets, and a picnic area at the trailhead.
- 7.2–11.5-mile loop, modest elevation change, 3.5–7 hours.
- Most of the trail is flat with some hilly regions.
- Dirt, rocks, sand, old pavement – suitable for older children.
- Head west along the Three Brothers rock formation base, past Camp 4 to El Capitan. For the 7.2-mile loop, cross El Capitan Bridge over Merced River here and head back eastward toward the village.
- To hike the full 11.5-mile loop, continue past El Capitan west toward Bridalveil Fall before looping back around toward the village.

Sentinel Dome and Taft Point Loop – Yosemite Valley

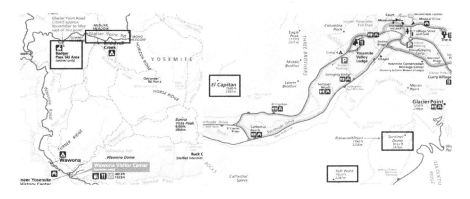

- The trailhead is signed as Sentinel Dome off Glacier Point Road with pullout parking to the right; accessible via Wawona Road past the Wawona Visitor Center close to the South entrance.
- 4.9-mile loop trail, 1,000 feet elevation change, 3–4 hours.
- Start with a stroll through the woodlands to the granite dome, which has breathtaking 360° views of the valley and offers a close encounter with El Capitan, a 3,000-foot granite monolith.
- After taking in the views, walk down and turn left to join Pohono trail.
- The final part of the trail is a mixture of meadows and pine forests. Cross Sentinel Creek before reaching Taft Point and The Fissures.

Be extra careful around these landmarks. While the granite fractures are intriguing, there are sheer drops and no railings.

- Hike later in the day to watch the sunset over the giant rock formations, but don't forget your flashlight.
- In winter, Glacier Point Road is closed, but you can park further away and access the trail with snowshoes or cross-country skis. When Badger Pass Ski Area is open from mid-December–March, Glacier Point Road is better prepped for cross-country skiing.

Columbia Rock Trail – Yosemite Valley

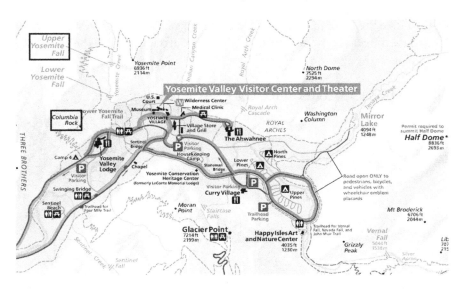

- From Camp 4 off Northside Drive, the trail begins from Upper Yosemite Falls trailhead. There is parking adjacent to the campground, or take the shuttle to stop #7: _Yosemite shuttle_.
- 2 miles out-and-back, 1,000 feet elevation change, 2–3 hours.
- Prepare for some pretty intense switchbacks at the start, and then the trail narrows to a single-track path.
- Watch your footing as you head up Columbia Rock. You don't need to hike all the way to the top as you can turn around at any point.
- The elevation allows sweeping views of the valley, the peaks of Sierra Nevada, Glacier Point, Half Dome, and North Dome.
- This is an extremely popular trail, so it is best to hike it during the week or early in the morning.

- Though you can hike here year-round, the trail may be covered with snow in winter through early spring, so be careful in icy conditions.

Advanced Trails

<u>Vernal and Nevada Falls via Mist Trail – Yosemite Valley</u>

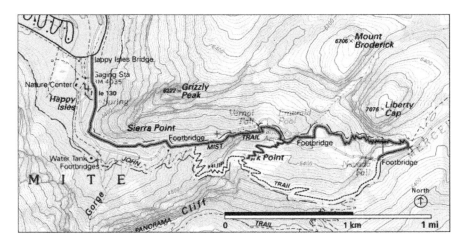

- Take the Happy Isles Loop Road and Mist trailhead to begin this hike. The parking lot is east of Curry Village.
- 5.4-mile lollipop loop, 2,000 feet elevation change, 5–6 hours.
- Partially paved – suitable for older children.
- From Mist trailhead, follow John Muir trail south passing Happy Isles Nature Center onto the Vernal Falls footbridge that takes you over Merced River with a view of Vernal Falls. Take advantage of the toilets and fountains here.
- At the first intersection keep left to start the ascent up the cliffside. Head past Emerald Falls to reach Nevada Falls. The loop meets Mist trail before heading back.
- From the high point at Nevada Falls you can take an alternative route that includes views of Liberty Cap in the distance.
- There is a granite slide into Emerald Pool, however, avoid the temptation as the underwater current is stronger than it looks.
- The mist from the waterfalls is refreshing but watch out for slippery paths underfoot.

- This is another hike that has a little bit of everything from forests to waterfalls, wildflowers to wildlife.
- Grab refreshments at Curry Village close to the trailhead before or after your hike.

Upper Yosemite Falls Trail – Yosemite Valley

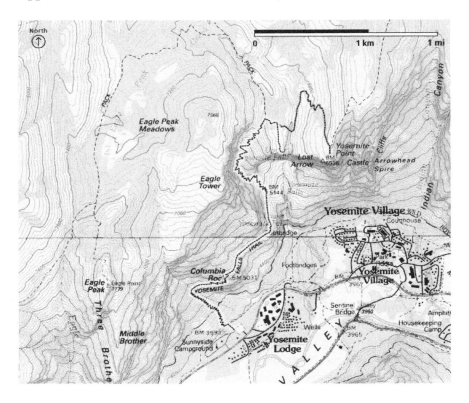

- Begin at Camp 4 off Northside Drive to find Upper Yosemite Falls trailhead.
- 7.2 miles out-and-back, 2,700 feet elevation change, 6–8 hours.
- Begins with intense switchbacks to Colombia Rock before heading northeast along the granite cliffside. After the metal gate there will be some scrambling and then another gate.
- Past the second gate you will overlook the falls with indescribable views and then retrace your steps.
- Be prepared for a total of 135 switchbacks on this steep hike.

- The lower gate has the best viewpoint for photos of the fall from below. There is a section here that is flat for 500 feet, which is a good resting point.
- A staircase with a guardrail climbs to the overlook of the falls, which is adrenalizing for those not scared of heights.
- Yosemite Falls is the tallest waterfall in North America and the 6th tallest in the world. The views from the top are out of this world!

Half Dome via the John Muir Trail – Yosemite Valley

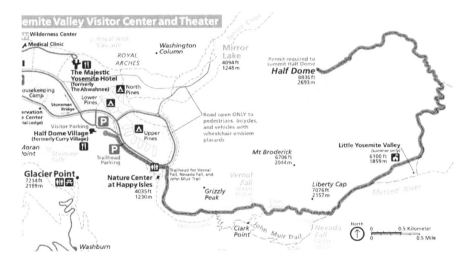

- Start at Happy Isles trailhead. There is parking ½ mile away at Curry Village.
- 16.5 miles out-and-back, 4,836 feet elevation change, 8–10 hours.
- At the first intersection, take the John Muir trail. Although it's slightly longer, it's a gentler incline. Pass Little Yosemite campsite before climbing up to the Half Dome trail.
- From here it's only 2 more miles to the summit beginning with carved out stairs in the granite before the final 0.25 miles using bolted cables. This section alone can take an hour, and sturdy shoes are a must.
- Obtain a _permit_ for the Half Dome summit.
- The first part of the trail is nicely shaded with black oak and mixed conifers. There are also wildflowers and a chance to see wildlife, especially birds and big game.

- The highlight is the park views including Liberty Cap, Nevada Falls, and the 360° views of Sierra Nevada at the summit.
- Break up the hike by camping at Little Yosemite camp or at the Cloud's Rest trail.
- Parts of the trail are suitable for horseback riding.

There is so much history and fun in Yosemite National Park. It's great for families, and despite the large crowds, if you time things well you can enjoy the tranquility as you marvel at the towering granite structures and some of the most beautiful waterfalls you can imagine. It's also a park with an excellent range of facilities, especially for those with disabilities. Nobody is excluded from this immense park and its views.

CONCLUSION

When looking at these mind-blowing parks and the true power of nature, it's easy to forget one of the fundamental aspects of hiking. These parks are visited by hundreds and thousands of people in any given month. For the parks to remain an abundance of joy for all, we must all respect the environment and follow the 'Leave no Trace' rule.

"What we are doing to the forests of the world is a mirror reflection of what we are doing to ourselves and one another."

— *CHRIS MASER*

The Leave No Trace seven principles aren't just in place for us humans to continue enjoying the wilderness; they are there to protect wildlife and vegetation. You only have to look at the amount of plastic we have dumped into the ocean or air pollution to appreciate the extensive damage we can cause.

Here is an overview of the seven principles:

1. Plan ahead and prepare.

We have done plenty of planning and preparation in this book, so this should help you schedule your visits and hikes so that you get the most out of them and avoid times of high traffic. If you are traveling in larger groups, try splitting up to minimize any impact.

2. Travel and camp on durable surfaces.

There is no need to alter a site for camping when you can easily find one that is ready. If you see areas with signs of other campers, avoid this to prevent the creation of new campsites. Stick to harder surfaces and remain 200 feet from lakes and streams.

3. Dispose of waste properly.

Follow the rule of "Pack it in, Pack it out." What comes with you must leave with you, and this means cleaning up spilled food as well as all trash. If you can't find a toilet, human waste needs to be buried 6–8 inches deep and 200 feet from water, camps, and trails.

4. Leave what you find.

As tempted as you are to take even the smallest of rocks home, imagine what would happen to Yosemite, for instance, after nearly 4 million artifacts were removed from the park each year! Leave rocks, plants, and other natural objects in order to preserve the past and allow others to enjoy them in the future.

5. Minimize campfire impacts.

If possible, use a lightweight stove for cooking rather than campfires. If campfires are allowed, use the right equipment, and make sure all wood is burned to ashes and that the fire is put out. Scatter ashes once cooled.

6. Respect wildlife.

Animals in the parks are used to their natural habitat, including food. You aren't helping them by offering your leftover sandwiches. Leaving food for the wildlife only exposes them to predators and damages their health. Observe critters at a healthy distance, but never follow them!

7. Be considerate of other visitors.

Be respectful of others who are trying to escape the same stressors that you are. Yield to others on the trail and step to the downhill side of a trail to let groups pass. Everyone is there to enjoy the sound of nature, so avoid making too much noise. Listen to nature's sounds, not your own voice.

The moment you embark on your first hike, regardless of the park, you will be swept away by the beauty of hiking in nature. My partner and I take every opportunity to visit both new and old parks and hikes because there is always more to explore. It's ironic because the physical demands of a challenging hike still leave you recharged to more effectively tackle the week of responsibilities and work.

My health has improved more than I ever could have imagined due to the combination of busting stress and physical activity. I sleep better, and this enables me to think with more clarity. I make fewer mistakes than I used to, and decision–making is easier.

Don't get me wrong, my phone is always with me because I want to capture all the memories we make on our adventures. Nevertheless, it's amazing how you will forget about the constantly distracting device in your pocket when you are facing the scenery these parks offer. The escape has given me the space to grieve my losses, understand life's bigger picture, and live to the fullest while I can.

Breaking away from the city and concrete, hiking has given me a new appreciation of the importance of taking care of our environment and planet. The lessons that nature teaches us don't just end when you pass the park gates; they come with you and motivate you to do more from your home.

There is only one thing left for you to do, and ironically, it may be harder than the first trail you tackle — it's time to pick where to start! While this book is highly detailed, don't forget to check the park's website before heading out. As the climate changes so dramatically, no one can predict weather changes that can cause closures. Once your trail is selected, gather all you need for a safe hike and set off on your own adventure.

If I could ask one small favor of you, it would be for a review on Amazon. Trust me, this is not to boost my ego, although I do love hearing about all the fun you have had on your hikes. Sharing your reviews on Amazon is a great way to let others know that there is the right, informative guidebook so that they, too, can benefit from hiking in the Southwest. The more people who have access to detailed information, the better all of our hiking experiences will be!

Be safe, have fun, make memories, and hike to your heart's content!

There are numerous helpful web resources that have been researched and included in this book. To access all links compiled per park click or scan below bearing in mind that the formatting may look a little different on your phone.
URL: https://docs.google.com/document/d/1Uv0NeYZhxiYGXs5stqdZVAFOyRiZc YDronoyyAnvhuY/edit?usp=sharing

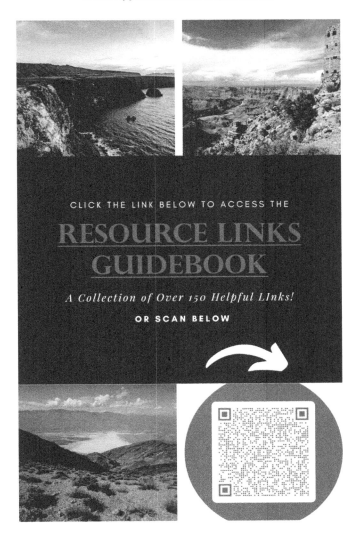

CLICK THE LINK BELOW TO ACCESS THE

RESOURCE LINKS
GUIDEBOOK

A Collection of Over 150 Helpful LInks!

OR SCAN BELOW

People Need to Hear Your Thoughts!

As I sit and look through photos of my hikes and the wonderful memories I have made with friends and family, all I want to do is encourage more and more people to get the most out of their time and their health by hiking in national parks. Now that you share this passion, I hope you can help spread the word.

As much as I love to hear about your exciting trips, others need to know that they can safely enjoy our national parks, regardless of their age or abilities. Just a moment of your time can give all others all the reassurance they need! Thank you, and I can't wait to see you for Southwest National Parks Volume II!

REFERENCES

29 Palms Resort - Home. (n.d.). http://www.twentyninepalmsresort.com/

About JTMF – Joshua Tree Music Festival. (n.d.). https://joshuatreemusicfestival.com/about-jtmf/

A Guide To Zabriskie Point | Death Valley National Park | 10Adventures. (n.d.). 10 Adventures https://www.10adventures.com/hikes/death–valley/zabriskie–point/

A quote from Travels with Charley. (n.d.). https://www.goodreads.com/quotes/445097–the–redwoods–once–seen–leave–a–mark–or–create–a#

Achilli, F. (n.d.). *Congress Trail Map, Sequoia.* Flickr. https://www.flickr.com/photos/travelourplanet/29513749946

Advice from a Saguaro | Floating Petals Monday's Flower Quote. (2019, August 8). Floating Petals. https://floatingpetals.com/flower–quote–advice–from–a–saguaro/

Ah–Pah Interpretive Trail | A Short, Scenic Adventure | 10Adventures. (n.d.). 10Adventures. https://www.10adventures.com/hikes/redwoods–national–and–state–parks/ah–pah–interpretive–trail/

Albuquerque International Sunport – gateway of New Mexico. (2024, January 2). ABQ Sunport. https://www.abqsunport.com/

Alerts & Conditions - Lassen Volcanic National Park (U.S. National Park Service). (n.d.). https://www.nps.gov/lavo/planyourvisit/conditions.htm

All Trails. (n.d.–b). *Del Norte Trail and Navy Road loop.* https://www.alltrails.com/explore/trail/us/california/del–norte–trail–and–navy–road–loop?mobileMap=false&ref=sidebar–static–map&u=m

All Trails. (n.d.–c). *General Grant trail.* https://www.alltrails.com/trail/us/california/general–grant–trail?u=m

All Trails. (n.d.–d). *Glacier Point trail.* https://www.alltrails.com/trail/us/california/glacier–point–trail?u=m

All Trails. (n.d.–e). *Lower Yosemite Falls trail.* https://www.alltrails.com/trail/us/california/lower–yosemite–falls–trail?u=m

All Trails. (n.d.–f). *Mica View–Cholla–Cactus Forest loop trail.* https://www.alltrails.com/trail/us/arizona/mica–view–loop–trail?u=m

All Trails. (n.d.–g). *Mill Creek Horse trail.* https://www.alltrails.com/trail/us/california/rellim–ridge–trail?u=m

All Trails. (n.d.–h). *Mirror Lave via Valley Loop trail.* https://www.alltrails.com/trail/us/california/mirror–lake–via–valley–loop–trail?u=m

All Trails. (n.d.–i). *Montañon Ridge loop.* https://www.alltrails.com/trail/us/california/montanon–ridge–loop?u=m

All Trails. (n.d.–j). *Onyx Bridge trail.* https://www.alltrails.com/trail/us/arizona/onyx–bridge–trail?u=m

All Trails. (n.d.–k). *Painted Desert Rim trail.* https://www.alltrails.com/trail/us/arizona/painted–desert–rim–trail?u=m

All Trails. (n.d.–l). *Potato Harbor.* https://www.alltrails.com/trail/us/california/potato–harbor?u=m

All Trails. (n.d.–m). *Prewett Point trail.* https://www.alltrails.com/explore/recording/prewett–point–trail––2?u=m

All Trails. (n.d.–n). *Ride Lake trail.* https://www.alltrails.com/trail/us/california/ridge–lakes–trail?u=m

All Trails. (n.d.–o). *Split Rock loop*. https://www.alltrails.com/trail/us/california/split–rock–loop––4?u=m

All Trails. (n.d.–p). *Sulphur Works*. https://www.rockymountainhikingtrails.com/devils–kitchen.htm

All Trails. (n.d.–q). *Zumwalt Meadow and Roaring River Falls*.

Amtrak. (n.d.). http://www.amtrak.com/

Anacapa Island hiking map. (n.d.). https://ontheworldmap.com/usa/national–park/channel–islands/anacapa–island–hiking–map.html

Apache stables. (n.d.). http://www.apachestables.com/

Arizona-Sonora Desert Museum, Tucson, AZ - Zoo, Botanical Garden and Art Gallery. (n.d.). https://www.desertmuseum.org/

Authority, T. A. (n.d.). *Tucson International Airport (TUS) | Fly Tucson*. Fly Tucson. https://www.flytucson.com/

Auto Touring - Yosemite National Park (U.S. National Park Service). (n.d.). https://www.nps.gov/yose/planyourvisit/touring.htm

Backcountry Camping - Lassen Volcanic National Park (U.S. National Park Service). (n.d.). https://www.nps.gov/lavo/planyourvisit/wilderness-permit-information.htm

Backcountry camping online permits - Redwood National and State Parks (U.S. National Park Service). (n.d.). https://www.nps.gov/redw/planyourvisit/backcountrypermits.htm

Backcountry permit - Grand Canyon National Park (U.S. National Park Service). (n.d.). https://www.nps.gov/grca/planyourvisit/backcountry-permit.htm

Basic information - Channel Islands National Park (U.S. National Park Service). (n.d.-a). https://www.nps.gov/chis/planyourvisit/basicinfo.htm

Basic information - Channel Islands National Park (U.S. National Park Service). (n.d.-b). https://www.nps.gov/chis/planyourvisit/basicinfo.htm

Basin Transit – Transit Serving the Communities of the Morongo Basin for over 20 years. (n.d.). https://basin-transit.com/

Be a B.A.R.K. Ranger - PETs (U.S. National Park Service). (n.d.). https://www.nps.gov/subjects/pets/be-a-bark-ranger.htm

Bernal, S. (2019). Pinnacles National Park: Bear Gulch to High Peaks Loop. *We Who Roam*. https://wewhoroam.com/pinnacles–national–park–bear–gulch–to–high–peaks–loop/

Bicycling - Petrified Forest National Park (U.S. National Park Service). (n.d.). https://www.nps.gov/pefo/planyourvisit/bicycling.htm

Bicycling at Saguaro National Park - Saguaro National Park (U.S. National Park Service). (n.d.). https://www.nps.gov/sagu/planyourvisit/bicycling-at-saguaro-national-park.htm

Bicycling in the Redwoods - Redwood National and State Parks (U.S. National Park Service). (n.d.). https://www.nps.gov/redw/planyourvisit/bikes.htm

Big Baldy Ridge route. (n.d.). Trail Forks. https://www.trailforks.com/route/big–baldy–ridge/

Bignell, R. (n.d.). *Photo/map album of Cavern Point Loop Trail*. http://hikeswithtykes.blogspot.com/2013/09/photo–map–album–of–cavern–point–loop.html

Biking & Bike Rentals | Yosemite National Park CA | TravelYosemite.com. (n.d.). Yosemite. https://www.travelyosemite.com/things-to-do/biking/

Biking - Joshua Tree National Park (U.S. National Park Service). (n.d.). https://www.nps.gov/jotr/planyourvisit/mountain-biking.htm

Biking & Mountain Biking - Death Valley National Park (U.S. National Park Service). (n.d.). https://www.nps.gov/deva/planyourvisit/bikingandmtbiking.htm

BirdShooter. (2012, January 27). *Shoshone Point trail map*. N2Backpacking | BirdShooter's Backpacking Blog & Podcast Series.

Bird Watching - Pinnacles National Park (U.S. National Park Service). (n.d.). https://www.nps.gov/pinn/planyourvisit/bird-watching.htm

Birds - Pinnacles National Park (U.S. National Park Service). (n.d.). https://www.nps.gov/pinn/learn/nature/birds.htm

Black Rock Canyon - Joshua Tree National Park (U.S. National Park Service). (n.d.). https://www.nps.gov/jotr/planyourvisit/blackrock.htm

Boyden Cavern. (n.d.). Boyden Cavern. https://boydencavern.com/

Brahan, C. (2021). Gould Mine Trail in Saguaro National Park. *Just Go Travel Studios.* https://www.justgotravelstudios.com/blogs/just-go-travel-blog/gould-mine-trail-saguaro-national-park

Brahan, C. (2022). Lady Bird Johnson Grove Trail in Redwood National Park. *Just Go Travel Studios.* https://www.justgotravelstudios.com/blogs/just-go-travel-blog/lady-bird-johnson-grove-trail-redwood-national-park

Brahan, P. (2018). Blue Mesa Trail in Petrified Forest National Park. *Just Go Travel Studios.* https://www.justgotravelstudios.com/blogs/just-go-travel-blog/just-go-to-petrified-forest-national-park-hiking-the-blue-mesa-trail

Brahan, P. (2019). Bumpass Hell Trail in Lassen Volcanic National Park. *Just Go Travel Studios.* https://www.justgotravelstudios.com/blogs/just-go-travel-blog/bumpass-hell-trail-lassen-volcanic-national-park

Brahan, P. (2020). Valley View Overlook trail in Saguaro National Park. *Just Go Travel Studios.* https://www.justgotravelstudios.com/blogs/just-go-travel-blog/valley-view-overlook-trail-saguaro-national-park

Bridal Wreath Falls and Canyon, Saguaro National Park. (n.d.). https://debravanwinegarden.blogspot.com/2019/01/bridal-wreath-falls-and-canyon-saguaro.html

Cabin, P. D. R. (n.d.). *Painted Desert Ranger Cabin.* Painted Desert Ranger Cabin. https://painteddesertrangercabin.com/

Cactus Garden Trail (U.S. National Park Service). (n.d.). https://www.nps.gov/places/cactus-garden-trail.htm

Campgrounds - Joshua Tree National Park (U.S. National Park Service). (n.d.). https://www.nps.gov/jotr/planyourvisit/campgrounds.htm

Camping - Channel Islands National Park (U.S. National Park Service). (n.d.). https://www.nps.gov/chis/planyourvisit/camping.htm

Camping - Grand Canyon National Park (U.S. National Park Service). (n.d.). https://www.nps.gov/grca/planyourvisit/camping.htm

Camping - Lassen Volcanic National Park (U.S. National Park Service). (n.d.). https://www.nps.gov/lavo/planyourvisit/camping-in-campgrounds.htm

Camping - Saguaro National Park (U.S. National Park Service). (n.d.). https://www.nps.gov/sagu/planyourvisit/camping.htm#:

Camping - Sequoia & Kings Canyon National Parks (U.S. National Park Service). (n.d.). https://www.nps.gov/seki/planyourvisit/campgrounds.htm

Camping at Pinnacles - Pinnacles National Park (U.S. National Park Service). (n.d.). https://www.nps.gov/pinn/planyourvisit/camp.htm

Camping in Death Valley - Death Valley National Park (U.S. National Park Service). (n.d.). https://www.nps.gov/deva/planyourvisit/camping-in-death-valley.htm

Camping options - Redwood National and State Parks (U.S. National Park Service). (n.d.). https://www.nps.gov/redw/planyourvisit/camping.htm

Camping – Channel Islands National Park (U.S. National Park Service). (n.d.). https://www.nps.gov/chis/planyourvisit/camping.htm

CBS San Francisco. (2014, June 30). Our favorite quotes about Yosemite – 150 years after federal protection. *CBS News.* https://www.cbsnews.com/sanfrancisco/news/our-favoirte-quotes-about-yosemite-150-years-after-federal-protection/#

Chamberlain, D. (2015, May 18). *The blue dot report's Dave Schlom: Lassen celebrates 100-year anniversary of its great eruption, and we're invited.* https://anewscafe.com/2015/05/18/ redding/dave–schlom–q–and–a/

Channel Islands National Marine Sanctuary. (n.d.). https://channelislands.noaa.gov/

Channel Islands National Park, California - Recreation.gov. (n.d.). Recreation.gov. https://www. recreation.gov/camping/gateways/2631

Channel Islands National Park (U.S. National Park Service). (n.d.). https://www.nps.gov/chis/ index.htm

Choice Hotels - please use a supported browser. (n.d.). https://www.choicehotels.com/arizona/ tucson/saguaro-national-park-
hotels

City of Visalia - airport. (n.d.). https://www.visalia.city/depts/transportation_services/airport/ default.asp

Climbing - Pinnacles National Park (U.S. National Park Service). (n.d.). https://www.nps.gov/pinn/ planyourvisit/climb.htm

Collection item (U.S. National Park Service). (n.d.–a). https://www.nps.gov/media/photo/ collection–item.htm?pg=7347320&cid=305fb7af–a71b–469b–941e– a98b439c882f&id=dd2e2a37–1ec5–4f86–939c–4d37d9136657&sid=5917b8cb– ba4a42279e6d5db7e309c74a&p=1&sort=

Collection item (U.S. National Park Service). (n.d.–b). https://www.nps.gov/media/photo/ collection–item.htm?pg=7347320&cid=305fb7af–a71b–469b–941e– a98b439c882f&id=dd2e2a37–1ec5–4f86–939c–4d37d9136657&sid=51bda2c3f7f54c5b– b3f7b82f20a48f8b&p=1&sort=

Collection item (U.S. National Park Service). (n.d.–c). https://www.nps.gov/media/photo/ collection–item.htm?pg=7347320&cid=305fb7af–a71b–469b–941e– a98b439c882f&id=dd2e2a37–1ec5–4f86–939c–4d37d9136657&sid=51bda2c3f7f54c5b– b3f7b82f20a48f8b&p=1&sort=

Compos, J. (2020). Hike Rincon Peak via the Miller Creek Trail #28 – Tucson, Arizona. *DownTheTrail.com.* https://www.downthetrail.com/exploring–arizona/hike–rincon–peak– miller–creek–trail–28–tucson–arizona/

Cook's Meadow Loop – Yosemite National Park (U.S. National Park Service). (n.d.). https://www.nps. gov/yose/planyourvisit/cooksmeadowtrail.htm

Dantes View (U.S. National Park Service). (n.d.). https://nps.gov/places/dantes-view.htm

Dark Sky Festival - Lassen Volcanic National Park (U.S. National Park Service). (n.d.). https://www. nps.gov/lavo/planyourvisit/dark-sky.htm

Death Valley entrance Fees - Death Valley National Park (U.S. National Park Service). (n.d.). https:// www.nps.gov/deva/planyourvisit/fees.htm

Death Valley National Park (U.S. National Park Service). (n.d.). https://www.nps.gov/deva/ index.htm

Death Valley Map. (n.d.). http://www.destination360.com/north–america/us/california/death– valley–national–park–map

Delagran, L. (n.d.). *How does nature impact our wellbeing?* Taking Charge of Your Health & Wellbeing. https://www.takingcharge.csh.umn.edu/how–does–nature–impact– our–wellbeing

Del Norte County Regional Airport | Fly Crescent City. (n.d.). Flycrescentcity. https://www. flycrescentcity.com/

DesertUSA.com. (n.d.). *Petrified Forest NP Location– Maps.* https://www.desertusa.com/pet/ du_pet_map.html

Directions – Petrified Forest National Park (U.S. National Park Service). (n.d.). https://www.nps.gov/ pefo/planyourvisit/directions.htm

Directions to the park – Saguaro National Park (U.S. National Park Service). (n.d.). https://www.nps.

gov/sagu/planyourvisit/directionstothepark.htm

Directions & Transportation – Joshua Tree National Park (U.S. National Park Service). (n.d.). https://www.nps.gov/jotr/planyourvisit/directions.htm

Directions & Transportation – Sequoia & Kings Canyon National Parks (U.S. National Park Service). (n.d.). https://www.nps.gov/seki/planyourvisit/directions.htm

Eating & Sleeping - Petrified Forest National Park (U.S. National Park Service). (n.d.). https://www.nps.gov/pefo/planyourvisit/eatingsleeping.htm

Elliott, K. (2023, December 18).

Entrance fees & passes - Sequoia & Kings Canyon National Parks (U.S. National Park Service). (n.d.). https://www.nps.gov/seki/planyourvisit/fees.htm

Entrance passes (U.S. National Park Service). (n.d.). https://www.nps.gov/planyourvisit/passes.htm

FAQ. (n.d.). Hiking Project. https://www.hikingproject.com/help/21/overview-of-site-name-features

Fees & Passes - Grand Canyon National Park (U.S. National Park Service). (n.d.). https://www.nps.gov/grca/planyourvisit/fees.htm

Fees & passes - Joshua Tree National Park (U.S. National Park Service). (n.d.). https://www.nps.gov/jotr/planyourvisit/fees.htm

Fees & passes - Lassen Volcanic National Park (U.S. National Park Service). (n.d.). https://www.nps.gov/lavo/planyourvisit/fees.htm

Fees & passes - Petrified Forest National Park (U.S. National Park Service). (n.d.). https://www.nps.gov/pefo/planyourvisit/fees.htm

Fees & passes - Pinnacles National Park (U.S. National Park Service). (n.d.). https://www.nps.gov/pinn/planyourvisit/fees.htm

Fees & Passes - Redwood National and State Parks (U.S. National Park Service). (n.d.). https://www.nps.gov/redw/planyourvisit/fees.htm

Fees & passes - Saguaro National Park (U.S. National Park Service). (n.d.). https://www.nps.gov/sagu/planyourvisit/fees.htm

Fees & Passes - Yosemite National Park (U.S. National Park Service). (n.d.). https://www.nps.gov/yose/planyourvisit/fees.htm

File:NPS Death-valley-regional-map.gif – Wikimedia Commons. (2013, October 21). https://commons.wikimedia.org/wiki/File:NPS_death-valley-regional-map.gif

File:NPS grand-canyon-north-rim-visitor-center-map.jpg – Wikimedia Commons. (2016, May 15). https://commons.wikimedia.org/wiki/File:NPS_grand-canyon-north-rim-visitor-center-map.jpg

File:NPS joshua-tree-hidden-valley-trail-map.gif. (2014, January 11). Wikimedia Commons. https://commons.wikimedia.org/wiki/File:NPS_joshua-tree-hidden-valley-trail-map.gif

Fish - Redwood National and State Parks (U.S. National Park Service). (n.d.). https://www.nps.gov/redw/learn/nature/fish.htm

Fishing - Yosemite National Park (U.S. National Park Service). (n.d.). https://www.nps.gov/yose/planyourvisit/fishing.htm

Foothills hikes in Sequoia National Park. (n.d.). The Fresno Bee. https://www.fresnobee.com/sports/outdoors/article19499367.html

Fresno Yosemite International Airport. (2023b, November 13). *Fresno Yosemite International Airport*. Fresno Yosemite International Airport | FAT | Fresno, CA. https://flyfresno.com/

Furnace Creek, CA. (n.d.). https://digital-desert.com/furnace-creek-ca/

Furnace Creek Campground, Death Valley National Park - Recreation.gov. (n.d.). Recreation.gov. https://www.recreation.gov/camping/campgrounds/232496?tab=seasons

Geology Tour Road. (n.d.). http://digital-desert.com/joshua-tree-national-park/geology-tour-road/

Golden Canyon, Gower Gulch, & Badlands – Death Valley National Park (U.S. National Park Service).

(n.d.). https://www.nps.gov/deva/planyourvisit/golden-canyon.htm

Grand Canyon. (2023, December 19). *Grand Canyon Lodging & Attractions - Visit Grand Canyon.* http://www.visitgrandcanyon.com/

Grand Canyon Kennel (U.S. National Park Service). (n.d.). https://www.nps.gov/places/000/grand-canyon-kennel.htm

Grand Canyon National Park (U.S. National Park Service). (n.d.). https://www.nps.gov/grca/index.htm

Grand Canyon Railway. (n.d.). *Grand Canyon Railway.* https://www.thetrain.com/

Greyhound: Affordable bus tickets across US, Canada & Mexico. (n.d.). https://www.greyhound.com/

Groome Transportation. (2023, November 30). *Airport shuttle service - Groome transportation - Book online.* https://groometransportation.com/

GuideAlong. (2023, August 30). *Grand Canyon South Rim Audio Driving Tour | GuideAlong.* https://gypsyguide.com/tour/grand-canyon-south-rim/

Half dome permits for day hikers - Yosemite National Park (U.S. National Park Service). (n.d.). https://www.nps.gov/yose/planyourvisit/hdpermits.htm

Happy Isles Art and Nature Center (U.S. National Park Service). (n.d.). https://www.nps.gov/places/000/happy-isles-art-and-nature-center.htm

Harry Reid International Airport. (n.d.). https://www.harryreidairport.com/

Havasupai Falls. (n.d.). https://www.thecanyon.com/havasupai-falls

Hazzard, C. (2021a). Bright Angel Trail to Plateau Point hike. *HikingGuy.com.* https://hikingguy.com/hiking-trails/grand-canyon-hikes/bright-angel-trail-to-plateau-point-hike/

Hazzard, C. (2021b). Hike the South Kaibab Trail to Skeleton Point. *HikingGuy.com.* https://hikingguy.com/hiking-trails/grand-canyon-hikes/hike-the-south-kaibab-trail-to-skeleton-point/

Hazzard, C. (2022). Panorama loop and Warren Peak (Joshua Tree). *HikingGuy.com.* https://hikingguy.com/hiking-trails/joshua-tree-hikes/panorama-loop-and-warren-peak-joshua-tree/

Hiiker. (n.d.). *Jawbone Trail trail stages.* https://hiiker.app/trails/california/san-benito-county/jawbone-trail/stages

Hike Lost Palms Oasis trail. (2017, January 29). Outdoor Blueprint. https://outdoorblueprint.com/national-parks/joshua-tree/hike-lost-palms-oasis-trail/

Hike Ryan Mountain Trail. (2017, January 24). Outdoor Blueprint. https://outdoorblueprint.com/national-parks/joshua-tree/hike-ryan-mountain-trail/

Hike the Cinder Cone Trail. (2017, January 1). Outdoor Blueprint. https://outdoorblueprint.com/national-parks/lassen-volcanic/hike-cinder-cone-trail/

Hike to Kings Creek Falls (U.S. National Park Service). (n.d.). https://www.nps.gov/thingstodo/hikekingscreekfalls.htm

Hiking around Las Vegas, Death Valley NP, Telescope Peak area map. (n.d.). https://www.birdandhike.com/Hike/DEVA/Tele_Pk/map-tp/Tele_Map-O.htm

Hiking map for Devil's Playground Stav Is Lost. (n.d.). Stav Is Lost. https://www.stavislost.com/hikes/trail/devils-playground-petrified-forest/map

Hiking map for Wasson Peak via Sweetwater trail. (n.d.). Stav Is Lost. https://www.stavislost.com/hikes/trail/wasson-peak-via-sweetwater-trail/map

Hipcamp. (n.d.). *Find yourself outside | Discover the best camping near you.* http://www.hipcamp.com/

Home. (n.d.). https://flymfr.com/

Home - Bright Angel Bicycles. (2023, December 23). Bright Angel Bicycles. https://bikegrandcanyon.com/

Home - Palm Springs International Airport (PSP) - Palm Springs, California. Palm Springs International Airport (PSP) - Palm

Springs, California. https://flypsp.com/

Home - Sequoia Shuttle. (2024, January 9). Sequoia Shuttle. http://www.sequoiashuttle.com/

Home page | San Francisco International Airport. (2024, January 11). San Francisco International Airport. https://www.flysfo.com/

Home page | San José Mineta International Airport. (n.d.). https://www.flysanjose.com/

Horseback riding - Joshua Tree National Park (U.S. National Park Service). (n.d.). https://www.nps.gov/jotr/planyourvisit/horseback-riding.htm

Horseback Riding & Mule Rides | Yosemite National Park CA | TravelYosemite.com. (n.d.). Yosemite. https://www.travelyosemite.com/things-to-do/horseback-mule-riding/

Horseback riding - Petrified Forest National Park (U.S. National Park Service). (n.d.). https://www.nps.gov/pefo/planyourvisit/horseback-riding.htm

Horseback Riding Tours | Yosemite Trails Horseback Adventures. (n.d.). http://www.yosemitetrails.com/

Horsetail Fall - Yosemite National Park (U.S. National Park Service). (n.d.). https://www.nps.gov/yose/planyourvisit/horsetailfall.htm

How to get to Saguaro National Park in Tucson by Bus? (2023, December 27). https://moovitapp.com/index/en/public_transit-Saguaro_National_Park-Tucson_AZ-site_18595505-1670

Humboldt County Airport, CA. (n.d.). Official Website. https://www.flyacv.com/

Iana. (2020). Boy Scout trail, Joshua Tree National Park. *The Happy Packers*. https://thehappypackers.com/boy-scout-trail-joshua-tree-national-park-california/

Inside the park Lodging, hotels & accommodations | Grand Canyon. (2023, December 13). Grand Canyon. http://www.grandcanyonlodges.com/lodging/

Island Packers. (n.d.). *Island Packers*. https://islandpackers.com/

Joshua Tree Lake RV and Campground. (n.d.). Joshua Tree Lake RV and Campground. http://www.joshuatreelake.com/

Joshua Tree National Park (U.S. National Park Service). (n.d.). https://www.nps.gov/jotr/index.htm

Joshua Tree Shops — Visit Joshua Tree. (n.d.). Visit Joshua Tree. https://www.joshuatree.guide/local-shops

Kuhn, M. (2022). Fortynine Palms Oasis trail. *Right Kind of Lost*. https://www.rightkindoflost.com/fortynine-palms-oasis-trail/

Lassen Volcanic National Park trail and camping map. (n.d.). https://ontheworldmap.com/usa/national-park/lassen-volcanic/lassen-volcanic-trail-and-camping-map.html

Lassen Volcanic National Park (U.S. National Park Service). (n.d.). https://www.nps.gov/lavo/index.htm

LAX Official Site | Welcome to Los Angeles International Airport. (n.d.). https://www.flylax.com/

Lodging - Grand Canyon National Park (U.S. National Park Service). (n.d.). https://www.nps.gov/grca/planyourvisit/lodging.htm

Lodging & Hotels | Sequoia & Kings Canyon National Parks. (n.d.). https://www.visitsequoia.com/lodging

Lodging - North Rim - Grand Canyon National Park (U.S. National Park Service). (n.d.). https://www.nps.gov/grca/planyourvisit/lodging-nr.htm

Ltd, E. (2023, November 10). *Download SkyView Free App - EducationalAppStore*. Educational App Store. https://www.educationalappstore.com/app/skyview-free-explore-the-universe#:

Laura, & Laura. (2023). Guide to hiking Barker Dam Nature trail in Joshua Tree. *Fun Life Crisis*. https://funlifecrisis.com/barker-dam-nature-trail/

Lessard, K. (2022, October 4). Death Valley National Park: the complete guide. *Authentik Usa*. https://www.authentikusa.com/be-en/blog/death-valley-national-park-the-complete-guide

Maps – Grand Canyon National Park (U.S. National Park Service). (n.d.). https://www.nps.gov/grca/planyourvisit/maps.htm

Maps – Lassen Volcanic National Park (U.S. National Park Service). (n.d.–a). https://www.nps.gov/lavo/planyourvisit/maps.htm

Maps – Redwood National and State Parks (U.S. National Park Service). (n.d.). https://www.nps.gov/redw/planyourvisit/maps.htm

Maps – Saguaro National Park (U.S. National Park Service). (n.d.–a). https://www.nps.gov/sagu/planyourvisit/maps.htm

Maps – Sequoia & Kings Canyon National Parks (U.S. National Park Service). (n.d.). https://nps.gov/seki/planyourvisit/maps.htm

Maps – Yosemite National Park (U.S. National Park Service). (n.d.). https://www.nps.gov/yose/planyourvisit/maps.htm

Manzanita Lake Campground - Lassen Volcanic National Park (U.S. National Park Service). (n.d.). https://www.nps.gov/lavo/planyourvisit/manzanita-lake-campground.htm

Mariposa Airport Mariposa-Yosemite Arrivals and departures, parking, terminal, information. (n.d.). https://tickets.pl/en/avia. https://tickets.pl/en/avia/airport/RMY

Mead, M. N. (2008). Benefits of sunlight: A bright spot for human Health. *Environmental Health Perspectives, 116*(4). https://doi.org/10.1289/ehp.116-a160

Melissa. (2021). One day in Sequoia and Kings Canyon National Parks. *Dogwoods & Driftwood.* https://www.dogwoodsanddriftwood.com/one-day-in-kings-canyon-and-sequoia-national-parks/

Michelle Obama Quotes. (n.d.). BrainyQuote. https://www.brainyquote.com/quotes/michelle_obama_452278#:

Mirror Lake day hike. (n.d.). Sierra Day Hikes. http://www.sierradayhikes.com/yosemite/mirror_lake.html

Mist Falls route. (n.d.). Trail Forks. https://www.trailforks.com/route/mist-falls/

Moore, K. (2022, December 5). Which entrance to take into Yosemite National Park. *Parked In Paradise.* https://www.parkedinparadise.com/yosemite-national-park-entrance/

Morgan, M., & Morgan, K. (2022). Best hiking quotes: 74 quotes about the great outdoors. *Where Are Those Morgans.* https://wherearethosemorgans.com/best-outdoor-hiking-quotes-captions/

Moro Rock trail. (n.d.). The Weekend Warrior. https://www.weekendwarriorfresno.com/moro-rock

Mosaic Canyon – Death Valley National Park (U.S. National Park Service). (n.d.). https://www.nps.gov/deva/planyourvisit/mosaic-canyon.htm

Motel in Joshua Tree, California - Joshua Tree Ranch House - Hotel Joshua Tree, California - Motel in Joshua Tree. (n.d.). https://www.jtrhmotel.com/

Mount Gould 07/25/2021. (2021, July 28). TJ's Adventures. https://hikingwithtj.com/mount-gould-07-25-2021/

Mountain, I. (2015). Break away from this trivial world of men. *The Inertia.* https://www.theinertia.com/video/break-away-from-this-trivial-world-of-men/

Mt. Perry hike in Death Valley National Park. (2018, April 25). Nancy East. https://www.hopeandfeathertravels.com/mt-perry-hike-in-death-valley-national-park/

Mule Trips - Grand Canyon National Park (U.S. National Park Service). (n.d.). https://www.nps.gov/grca/planyourvisit/mule_trips.htm

Murdock, M. (2023a, January 17). *Manzanita Lake Activities - Lassen Lodging.* Lassen Lodging. https://lassenlodging.com/manzanita-lake-activities/

Murdock, M. (2023b, July 14). *Drakesbad Guest Ranch - Lassen Lodging.* Lassen Lodging. https://lassenlodging.com/drakesbad/

Murdock, M. (2023c, December 20). *Death Valley Hotel | Death Valley Hotels | Hotels near Death Valley.* Stovepipe Wells Village. https://deathvalleyhotels.com/

National Park Foundation. (2022, November 8). *Channel Islands National Park*. https://www.nationalparks.org/explore/parks/channel–islands–national–park

National Park Maps | NPMaps.com – just free maps, period. (n.d.). National Park Maps. https://npmaps.com/

Northern region. (n.d.). https://wildlife.ca.gov/Regions/1

North Kaibab trail. (n.d.). Grand Canyon Conservancy. https://www.grandcanyon.org/park–information/trails/north–kaibab–trail/

nps.gov/submerged : Submerged Resources Center, National Park Service, Denver, Colorado. (n.d.). https://www.nps.gov/submerged/parks/chis.html

Off the beaten path—Blue Forest trail. (n.d.). https://www.nps.gov/pefo/off–the–beaten–path–blue–forest–trail.htm

Operating Hours & Seasons - Pinnacles National Park (U.S. National Park Service). (n.d.). https://www.nps.gov/pinn/planyourvisit/hours.htm

Pack Animal Trails and Overnight Camps. (n.d.). https://www.nps.gov/redw/planyourvisit/upload/HorseTrails_SB_2021-508-2.pdf

Palm Springs/Joshua Tree KOA. (n.d.). https://koa.com/campgrounds/palm-springs/

Panamint Springs Resort. (n.d.). https://www.panamintsprings.com/

Panoramic Point day hike. (n.d.). http://www.sierradayhikes.com/kings_canyon/panoramic_point.html

Papillon. (n.d.). *Helicopter Grand Canyon Tours with Papillon* [Video]. Papillon. https://www.papillon.com/grand-canyon-national-park/?ref=gccom

Parking – South Rim Visitor Center and Village – Grand Canyon National Park (U.S. National Park Service). (n.d.). https://www.nps.gov/grca/planyourvisit/parking_sr.htm

Park Shuttles - Sequoia & Kings Canyon National Parks (U.S. National Park Service). (n.d.). https://www.nps.gov/seki/planyourvisit/parktransit.htm

Petrified Forest National Park (U.S. National Park Service). (n.d.). https://www.nps.gov/pefo/

Petrified Forest National Park (U.S. National Park Service). (n.d.). https://www.nps.gov/pefo/index.htm

Petrified Forest National Park – Crystal Forest trail. (n.d.). DWHIKE. https://www.dwhike.com/Hikes–in–the–West/Arizona–Hikes/Petrified–Forest–Crystal–Forest–Trail–AZ/

Petrified Forest National Park – Giant Logs trail. (n.d.). DWHIKE. https://www.dwhike.com/Hikes–in–the–West/Arizona–Hikes/Petrified–Forest–Giant–Logs–Trail–AZ/

Phi. (2019). Hiking Yosemite's Half Dome — hermes LAPIN. *Hermes LAPIN*. https://www.hermeslapin.com/blog/2019/10/18/hiking–half–dome

Phoenix Sky Harbor International Airport - Official site. (n.d.). Phoenix Sky Harbor International Airport. https://www.skyharbor.com/

Pinnacles Campground, Pinnacles National Park - Recreation.gov. (n.d.). Recreation.gov. https://www.recreation.gov/camping/campgrounds/234015

Pinnacles NP. (n.d.). https://ai.stanford.edu/~latombe/mountain/photo/united–states/pinnacles–jan–2022.htm

Pinnacles National Park (U.S. National Park Service). (n.d.). https://www.nps.gov/pinn/index.htm

Pinnacles Recreation Co. (n.d.). Pinnacles Recreation Co. https://www.visitpinnacles.com/

Plan your visit – Death Valley National Park (U.S. National Park Service). (n.d.). https://www.nps.gov/deva/planyourvisit

Plan your visit – Pinnacles National Park (U.S. National Park Service). (n.d.). https://www.nps.gov/pinn/planyourvisit

Publications – Petrified Forest National Park (U.S. National Park Service). (n.d.). https://www.nps.gov/pefo/learn/publications.htm

Public transportation - Yosemite National Park (U.S. National Park Service). (n.d.). https://www.nps.gov/yose/planyourvisit/publictransportation.htm

Rae Lakes Loop - Sequoia & Kings Canyon National Parks (U.S. National Park Service). (n.d.). https://www.nps.gov/seki/planyourvisit/rae-lakes-loop.htm

Rainbow Forest Museum - Petrified Forest National Park (U.S. National Park Service). (n.d.). https://www.nps.gov/pefo/learn/historyculture/rainbow-forest-museum.htm

Redding Regional Airport (RDD). (n.d.). https://www.cityofredding.gov/government/departments/airports/redding_regional_airport.php

Redwood Coast Transit - public transit for Del Norte County. (2024, January 5). Redwood Coast Transit Authority. http://redwoodcoasttransit.org/

Redwood National and State Parks (U.S. National Park Service). (n.d.). https://www.nps.gov/redw/index.htm

Reno-Tahoe International Airport. (2024, January 6). *Passenger information - Reno-Tahoe International Airport*. https://www.renoairport.com/

Reserve California. (n.d.). https://reservecalifornia.com/Web/

Rim to Rim Grand Canyon transportation for hikers. (n.d.). https://www.trans-canyonshuttle.com/

Rock Climbing - Yosemite National Park (U.S. National Park Service). (n.d.). https://www.nps.gov/yose/planyourvisit/climbing.htm

Rome2Rio. (n.d.). https://www.rome2rio.com/map/Los-Angeles/Joshua-Tree-National-Park

Sacramento International Airport (SMF). (n.d.). https://sacramento.aero/smf

Sacred Sands – Your magical Joshua Tree getaway and wedding awaits. (n.d.). https://www.sacredsands.com/

Saguaro NP--East--Desert Ecology trail. (n.d.). Birding Hotspots. https://birdinghotspots.org/hotspot/L1922540

Saguaro National Park (U.S. National Park Service). (n.d.). https://www.nps.gov/sagu/index.htm

Santa Cruz del Norte Backcountry, Channel Islands National Park - Recreation.gov. (n.d.). Recreation.gov. https://www.recreation.gov/camping/campgrounds/232499

Sarah. (2021). Hiking Taft Point to Sentinel Dome loop. *Our Infinite Earth*. https://ourinfiniteearth.com/hiking-taft-point-to-sentinel-dome/

Sequoia & Kings Canyon National Parks (U.S. National Park Service). (n.d.). https://www.nps.gov/seki/index.htm

Sequoia Parks Conservancy. (2023, October 13). *Crystal Cave - Sequoia Parks Conservancy*. https://sequoiaparksconservancy.org/adventure/crystal-cave/

Sequoia Parks Conservancy. (2024, January 2). *Adventures & Events - Sequoia Parks Conservancy*. https://www.sequoiaparksconservancy.org/pearlakewinterhut.html

Shahar, Y. (2022a, March 26). Death Valley Badwater. *Yiftahshahar*. https://www.yiftahshahar.com/2022/03/death-valley-badwater.html

Shahar, Y. (2022b, March 26). Death Valley– Mesquite Flat Sand Dunes. *Yiftahshahar*. https://www.yiftahshahar.com/2022/03/death-valley-mesquite-flat-sand-dunes.html

Sightseeing- Park Highlights - Death Valley National Park (U.S. National Park Service). (n.d.). https://www.nps.gov/deva/planyourvisit/sightseeing-park-highlights.htm

Smigelski, S. (2017, April 23). *Balconies Cave in Pinnacles National Park*. https://www.hikespeak.com/trails/balconies-cave-pinnacles-national-park/

South Rim shuttle bus routes: Winter 2023-2024 - Grand Canyon National Park (U.S. National Park Service). (n.d.). https://www.nps.gov/grca/planyourvisit/shuttle-buses.htm

Stables, G. G. (n.d.). *Grant Grove Stables*. Grant Grove Stables. https://grantgrovestables.com/

Staff, & Staff. (2021, July 19). *Grand Canyon shuttle buses at the South Rim*. Grand Canyon National Park Trips. https://www.mygrandcanyonpark.com/road-trips/airports-trains/grand-canyon-shuttle/

StartLogic. (n.d.). http://grandcanyonshuttles.com/index.html

Steady Containment of Santa Cruz Island Fire – Channel Islands National Park (U.S. National Park Service). (n.d.). https://www.nps.gov/chis/learn/news/pr033118.htm

Tall Trees Grove – Famous Redwoods. (n.d.). http://famousredwoods.com/tall_trees_grove/

Tall Trees Trailhead Day-Use Online Reservations - Redwood National and State Parks (U.S. National Park Service). (n.d.-a). https://www.nps.gov/redw/planyourvisit/talltreespermits.htm

Talus Caves. (n.d.). https://https:\www.nps.gov\pinn\learn\nature\cave.htm#

Tang, L. (2023). Rae Lakes loop, Kings Canyon National Park — Lily M. Tang. *Lily M. Tang*. https://www.lilymtang.com/blog/rae–lakes–loop

Tanque Verde Ridge trail. (2013, November 4). Tucson Hikes. https://tucsonhikes.wordpress.com/2013/11/04/tanque–verde–ridge–trail/

Telescope Peak – Death Valley National Park (U.S. National Park Service). (n.d.). https://www.nps.gov/deva/planyourvisit/telescope–peak.htm

The 21 best national park quotes for your next adventure. (2023). *RVing With Rex*. https://rvingwithrex.com/2023/04/20/the–21–best–national–park–quotes–for–your–next–adventure/

The American Southwest. (n.d.-a). *Topographic map of the Lakes trail, Sequoia National Park*. https://www.americansouthwest.net/california/sequoia/lakes–trail–map.html

The American Southwest. (n.d.-b). *Trillium Falls trail, Redwood National Park, California*. https://www.americansouthwest.net/california/redwood/trillium–falls–trail.html

The Castle House: Estate. (n.d.). https://www.thecastlehouseestate.com/

The Joshua Tree House. (2023, July 3). *The JTH Tucson - Saguaro National Park, Tucson, AZ - inn*. https://www.thejoshuatreehouse.com/tucson/

The Joshua Tree Inn | Joshua Tree National Park | Joshua Tree CA. (n.d.). https://www.joshuatreeinn.com/

The Oasis at Death Valley. (2024, January 10). *Official site - The Oasis at Death Valley*. The Oasis at Death Valley - Oasis in Death Valley National Park. https://www.oasisatdeathvalley.com/

The Redwood Creek trail. (n.d.). http://www.redwoodhikes.com/RNP/RedwoodCreek.html

The Yurok Loop. (n.d.). http://www.redwoodhikes.com/RNP/Yurok.html

Things to do - Channel Islands National Park (U.S. National Park Service). (n.d.). https://www.nps.gov/chis/planyourvisit/things2do.htm

Tickets & Fares - YARTS - public transit to Yosemite. (2023, August 7). YARTS - Public Transit to Yosemite. https://yarts.com/tickets-and-fares/#mammoth-hwy-120-395

Top 12 quotes about joshua tree. (n.d.). https://quotestats.com/topic/quotes–about–joshua–tree/

Tortajada, N. (2022). Ultimate guide to backpacking Santa Cruz Island in the Channel Islands. *The Adventure Dispatch*. https://theadventuredispatch.com/adventure/santa–cruz–island–backpacking/

Trail Difficulty Ratings – Randonnée Aventure. (n.d.). https://randonnee.ca/trail–difficulty–ratings/

Trail Forks. (n.d.). *Brokeoff Mountain hike trail*. Trailforks. https://www.trailforks.com/trails/brokeoff–mountain/

Tulare County Area Transit – Transportation for Tulare, Visalia, Dinuba, Porterville, and Delano. (n.d.). https://ridetcat.org/

Tuweep - Grand Canyon National Park (U.S. National Park Service). (n.d.). https://www.nps.gov/grca/planyourvisit/tuweep.htm

Valenti, M. (2016). How to choose the right hike. *ACTIVE.com*. https://www.active.com/outdoors/articles/how–to–choose–the–right–hike

Vawter, K. (2023). Ultimate Saguaro National Park outdoor adventure guide. *Bearfoot Theory*. https://bearfoottheory.com/saguaro–national–park/

Vernal Fall and Nevada Fall trails – Yosemite National Park (U.S. National Park Service). (n.d.). https://www.nps.gov/yose/planyourvisit/vernalnevadatrail.htm

Village Historic District - Grand Canyon National Park (U.S. National Park Service). (n.d.). https://

www.nps.gov/grca/learn/historyculture/historic-village.htm

Visit Oxnard. (n.d.). *Island Packers - Visit Oxnard.* https://visitoxnard.com/directory/island-packers/

Visitor Center Information - Saguaro National Park (U.S. National Park Service). (n.d.). https://www.nps.gov/sagu/planyourvisit/visitor-center-information.htm

Visitor centers - Joshua Tree National Park (U.S. National Park Service). (n.d.). https://www.nps.gov/jotr/planyourvisit/visitorcenters.htm

V-Line. (n.d.). https://ridevline.com/

ViraFlare. (n.d.). *Best hikes in Yosemite National Park [HIKING GUIDE] – ViraFlare.* Tripoto. https://www.tripoto.com/missouri/trips/best-hikes-in-yosemite-national-park-hiking-guide-viraflare-5da7a34c1d843

Weather – Death Valley National Park (U.S. National Park Service). (n.d.). https://www.nps.gov/deva/learn/nature/weather–and–climate.htm

Weather - Death Valley National Park (U.S. National Park Service). (n.d.). https://www.nps.gov/deva/learn/nature/weather-and-climate.htm#

White Tank Arch – Joshua Tree National Park. (n.d.). http://digital–desert.com/arch–rock/

Wilderness Permits & Reservations - Sequoia & Kings Canyon National Parks (U.S. National Park Service). (n.d.). https://www.nps.gov/seki/planyourvisit/wilderness_permits.htm

Wilderness River Adventures | Grand Canyon, Glen Canyon, Cataract Canyon Rafting. (n.d.). WildernessRiverAdventures. https://www.riveradventures.com/

Wojtanik, A. (2020a, January 5). *Condor Gulch – High Peaks trail loop (Pinnacles National Park, CA).* Live and Let Hike. https://liveandlethike.com/2020/01/05/condor–gulch–high–peaks–trail–loop–pinnacles–national–park–ca/

Wojtanik, A. (2020b, January 14). *Bear Gulch Cave – rim trail loop (Pinnacles National Park, CA).* Live and Let Hike. https://liveandlethike.com/2020/01/13/bear–gulch–cave–rim–trail–loop–pinnacles–national–park–ca/

Wojtanik, A. (2020c, January 15). *Manzanita Lake trail (Lassen Volcanic National Park, CA).* Live and Let Hike. https://liveandlethike.com/2017/10/16/manzanita–lake–trail–lassen–volcanic–national–park–ca/

Wojtanik, A. (2020d, July 29). *Lassen Peak trail (Lassen Volcanic National Park, CA).* Live and Let Hike. https://liveandlethike.com/2020/07/29/lassen–peak–trail–lassen–volcanic–national–park–ca/

Wojtanik, A. (2021, May 23). *Upper Yosemite Falls trail (Yosemite National Park, CA).* Live and Let Hike. https://liveandlethike.com/2021/05/23/upper–yosemite–falls–trail–yosemite–national–park–ca/

Wojtanik, A. (2022a, January 13). *Scorpion Canyon Loop Trail (Channel Islands National Park, CA).* Live and Let Hike. https://liveandlethike.com/2022/01/12/scorpion–canyon–loop–trail–channel–islands–national–park–ca/

Wojtanik, A. (2022b, January 27). *Wasson Peak Loop (Saguaro National Park, AZ).* Live and Let Hike. https://liveandlethike.com/2022/01/27/wasson–peak–loop–saguaro–national–park–az/

Wojtanik, A. (2022d, March 28). *Golden Canyon, Badlands Loop, and Gower Gulch Trail Loop, including Red Cathedral & Zabriskie Point (Death Valley National Park, CA).* Live and Let Hike. https://liveandlethike.com/2020/03/07/golden–canyon–badlands–loop–and–gower–gulch–trail–loop–including–red–cathedral–zabriskie–point–death–valley–national–park–ca/

Wojtanik, A. (2022e, May 26). *Balconies Cliffs – Balconies Cave trail loop (Pinnacles National Park, CA).* Live and Let Hike. https://liveandlethike.com/2022/05/25/balconies–cliffs–balconies–cave–trail–loop–pinnacles–national–park–ca/

Wojtanik, A. (2022f, May 26). *Juniper Canyon Trail to High Peaks loop (Pinnacles National Park, CA).*

Live and Let Hike. https://liveandlethike.com/2022/05/24/juniper–canyon–trail–to–high–peaks–loop–pinnacles–national–park–ca/

Yosemite Falls Trail – Yosemite National Park (U.S. National Park Service). (n.d.). https://www.nps.gov/yose/planyourvisit/yosemitefallstrail.htm

Yosemite Museum - Yosemite National Park (U.S. National Park Service). (n.d.). https://www.nps.gov/yose/learn/historyculture/yosemite-museum.htm

Yosemite National Park and human attractions. (n.d.). GeographyFieldWork. https://geographyfieldwork.com/YosemiteTourismAttractions.htm

Yosemite National Park | Lodging & Year round activities | TravelYosemite.com. (n.d.). Yosemite. https://www.travelyosemite.com/

Yosemite National Park, California - Recreation.gov. (n.d.). Recreation.gov. https://www.recreation.gov/camping/gateways/2991

Yosemite National Park (U.S. National Park Service). (n.d.). https://www.nps.gov/yose/index.htm

Yosemite Valley Loop Trail – Yosemite National Park (U.S. National Park Service). (n.d.). https://www.nps.gov/yose/planyourvisit/valleylooptrail.htm

Yukti. (2023, March 9). 100+ Death Valley Captions For Instagram (Puns + Slogans). *Travel With Me 24 X 7*. https://travelwithme247blog.com/death–valley–captions–for–instagram/

Zetterlind, V. (n.d.). *Shuttle service*. Redwood Adventures. https://redwoodadventures.com/shuttle-service/